A PAGE FALLS OPEN
Stories and Poems by Irish Writers

Compiled by:
Noel Boohan
Martina Browne
Anne Cahill
Michael C. Downes
Mary Foudy
Moira Greene
Pat Morris

Edited by: Moira Greene

Foreword by: Tom Collins, Centre for Adult Education, St. Patrick's College, Maynooth

Layout and Typesetting: Michael C. Downes
Additional Typesetting: Sean Downes

Cover Design: Time Design Ltd., Ennis

Co. Clare Reading and Writing Scheme

A PAGE FALLS OPEN

Published by
Co. Clare Reading and Writing Scheme
Springfield House
Harmony Row
Ennis, Co. Clare

Printed by
Colour Books Ltd.
105 Industrial Estate
Baldoyle
Dublin 13

ISBN 0-9521893-0-5

First Edition - September 1993

*A page falls open
and the reader's name
is there.
It always has been
and will be always...*

With special thanks to Philip Casey

Acknowledgements

Acknowledgements and thanks are due to a number of individuals and organisations for their contribution to the *Writers for Literacy Project.*

First, we are indebted to all the writers who sent us stories, poems, memoirs etc. The response was overwhelming, and while we were unable to include all contributions in this volume, we would like to sincerely thank everyone who responded to our request.

Second, we are very grateful for the financial assistance received towards publication costs from the following:

Clare Co. Council, Clare Vocational Education Committee, Electricity Supply Board of Ennis, Soroptimists International of Ennis & District, Guinness Ireland Ltd. and anonymous contributors.

We would also like to thank Tom Collins, Centre for Adult Education, St. Patrick's College, Maynooth; Geraldine Mernagh, Director, National Adult Literacy Agency; Patrick Gannon, Librarian, Sligo (formerly Ennis); Alf McLoughlan, Galway Literacy Scheme, Mary Togher, Organiser, Longford Literacy Scheme; Peadar MacNamara, Ennis Vocational School; and the staff at the Ennis Bookshop, for their advice and support.

The compilation of *"A Page Falls Open"* represents an enormous team effort involving the Co. Clare Reading and Writing Scheme, the Clare Unemployment Resource Centre, the Clare Vocational Training Opportunities Scheme, and the Adult Education Office. In addition to the compilers, others in Springfield House who helped with the project include: Mary Linnane, James Whyms, John Drinan, Brid Kennedy, Loretta Hughes, Orla Ní Eile, Jane Foley, Mary Ryan, Margaret McMahon, Dave Berry, Martina Callinan, Maura O'Donoghue, John Cusack, Maura Frawley, Martin O'Donoghue, Noel Phelan, Patricia Collins, Anne O'Connell, Mary Corry, Sandra Stackpoole, Evelyn Forde. We are grateful to all who supported us.

Finally, we would like to say a very special word of thanks to Sean Conlan, Adult Education Organiser, Co. Clare, for his advice, support, and encouragement throughout the project.

Foreword

Writing a foreword to a book with contributions from the range of literary luminaries contained in these pages, forcibly reminds me of the problem which confronted F. Scott Fitzgerald's anti-hero Anthony Patch in his search not "only for words in which to clothe thoughts but for thoughts worthy of being clothed." Nonetheless, on the basis that every privilege generates an equal and opposite headache, let me acknowledge my privilege at being associated with this publication, whatever about the accompanying headache of saying something meaningful.

Essentially this book is a celebration in which a range of literary figures from all over the country have participated. The book celebrates the achievements of the Co. Clare Reading and Writing Scheme, indeed of all adult literacy schemes, and acknowledges these achievements in the most appropriate manner imaginable - through the literary medium.

In a broader sense, this book is a further benchmark in the coming of age of the Adult Education Movement in Ireland. This movement is the great undocumented and even unobserved revolution of our times. However, unlike other so-called revolutions, this is not a revolution of new political structures or arrangements.

It is deeper and more fundamental than that. It is a

revolution of personal growth and liberation. It is a revolution in which the participants are shaping a new world both at a personal level and at a broader social level. It is a revolution which embraces a commitment to change and to becoming; to the triumph of light over darkness and to the power of hope over adversity. Essentially it is a revolution of the mind.

While it is invidious to refer to any one piece of work in this book, in the context of these observations it seems to me that Micheal O Siadhail's poem, *Sunflower*, is especially apt:

> "...*Tell me it's all worth this venture*
> *and I'll open a bloom, I'll flower at every chance.*
> *Then praise me all the way to the sky,*
> *Praise me with light, lover,*
> *Oh, praise me, praise me, praise me*
> *And I live forever.*"

TOM COLLINS
Centre for Adult Education
St. Patrick's College, Maynooth

CONTENTS

Sunflower
Micheal O'Siadhail

The danger of tautening towards the sun:
To lose is to lose all.
Too much gravity and I'm undone;
If I bend, I fall.

Tell me it's all worth this venture,
Just the slightest reassurance,
And I'll open a bloom, I'll flower
At every chance.

Then praise me all the way to the sky,
Praise me with light, lover,
Oh, praise me, praise me, praise me
And I live forever.

Hello

(For Emily, now that I've found her)
Michael Durack

On your maiden voyage
to the outside world
an icy winter blast
greeted you
at the hospital doorway,
while here and there a snowflake
hovered
in search of a landing place.

Next day I rode the snow-drifts
in a blizzard
homeward from work
to find you sleeping
in a Moses basket,
warmed by coal-fire
and mother-love.

Now there is summer sunshine
and rattlers
and plastic ducks
and gingham dresses

and conversations
(in your own dialect)
and smiles of recognition
and laughter in the mornings.

Do you know that on that Friday
afternoon as I rushed to greet
the news of your arrival
I passed you in the corridor?
Not knowing who you were,
I didn't even stop to say
HELLO.

Tiger's Bay

(from My Belfast Boyhood)
Sam McAughtry

I was born in Belfast in 1921.

My mother brought up ten of a family on her own, because my father was a merchant seaman, but when he came home from sea our house in Cosgrave Street was in a fine state of excitement. Our little house would be shining clean, and mother would be wearing a brand new pinny. She would have a little powder on her face and she would keep pulling and smoothing at her pinny, as the time for Dad's arrival grew closer.

After his ship was tied up in the dock, my father filled a bucket of hot water from a tap in the engine room. He carried this up onto the deck, and across to his quarters in the bows of the ship. He scrubbed himself pink-clean. Then he went, with his friend, the ship's lamptrimmer, to a pub in Whitla Street, near the dock entrance. The two of them would drink there for an hour or so, and then they would go home to their families.

Sometimes my father would arrive at the front door in a taxi. We kids thought it was all very splendid. I remember my wild excitement as I announced his arrival to mother, waiting in the kitchen.

When Dad stepped out of the taxi, I would rush to help with his long, white seaman's bag. There was always something in it for the youngsters: something from Canada or America or maybe Germany or Holland. From the streets all around Tiger's Bay the kids would come to marvel at the novelties my Dad had brought back from foreign parts.

Once my father brought something home for the whole family to play with. It was a long cart, called a Coaster Cart. It held four children, and it had four long handles which propelled the cart along when they were pushed and pulled, rather like one of those hand-driven railway buggies that used to appear in the funny pictures.

We had the most wonderful time with that Coaster Cart. Looking back on it, I think the real pleasure lay in the fact that it made us the centre of attention. The other kids used to line up, waiting for their turns for a ride. We McAughtrys felt like royalty, riding the cart whenever we liked. In the 1920s Tiger's Bay people didn't feel like royalty that often. It was no wonder we all loved our Dad so much.

His ship brought grain from America, or timber from the Baltic, or general cargo from Canada. Sometimes a part of this general cargo, in the early summer, would have been apples from Ontario, in Canada. Macintosh Reds, they were called. When the ship's hold was opened, those marvellous Macintosh Reds would fill the air with the most mouth watering scent I have ever known. When I first met that smell I was standing on the deck, looking down on the dockers just starting to unload the cases of apples. I couldn't help myself. "Hey, give us an apple, mister," I shouted to the nearest docker. A damaged case was lying beside him. He took one out of it and tossed it to me.

The skin of that Macintosh Red was the colour of a tomato, and it was as thin as tissue paper. As soon as my teeth met it the gorgeous juice flowed at twice the rate and five times the sweetness of the greeny-yellow local apples that were all I had known until then.

After the first bite it was clear that one apple wasn't going to be enough. I slid down the ladder and stood beside the docker. He was waving signals to the craneman. "If you want to go and do any messages or anything, I'll keep your place here," I said to him. He looked down at me.

"What age are you?" he wanted to know.

"Ten," I told him.

"What are you doing on board this ship?" he asked next.

"My daddy lives on this ship when he's not at home," I told him.

"Oh well, then," the docker said, "I beg your pardon for asking." He stood and thought for a while.

"I'll tell you what," he said finally. "Instead of you keeping my place here, why don't you mind these two damaged apples for me!" And bending down he took two more of the Macintosh Reds out of the broken case. Shoving them smartly up my jersey, I took off like a scalded cat up towards Tiger's Bay, before Dad told me off for corrupting dock labourers in the course of their duties.

In fact I used to spend a great deal of time at the waterfront. Ships were my whole life. In school I would sit and stare at my atlas and drift off in my mind to the North Atlantic, to the bridge of my father's ship, and I would pretend to be captain: Captain Sam McAughtry, the toughest old sea dog in the trade. In fact, I liked this title so much that I wrote it in all my school books. "This book is the property of Captain S.J. McAughtry." I might as well tell you, I carried the Captain business further than that. I used to send off for free samples advertised in the newspapers, signing myself Captain McAughtry.

Our postman wasn't too pleased about it. "You cut that out," he would say, "Or you'll get into trouble." But I only stopped it when a firm that made hair oil kept writing to me, asking when I was going to place my order. It gave me quite a fright: "They must think I own a shop or something," I said to myself. So I wrote a note to the company concerned. "Dear Sir," I wrote, "I am Captain McAughtry's solicitor. He doesn't want any more hair oil. Do not write any more letters or I will tell the police. Signed Captain Frankie Pattison."

Frankie Pattison was my best friend. He and I used to spend hours and hours together on the harbour estate after school. Sometimes we would take the ferryboat for a penny and cross the Spencer Basin to the shipyard.

We saw the beautiful pre-war passenger ships being built, like the great Union Castle liners, *Stirling Castle* and *Athlone Castle*. The huge funnel of the *Stirling Castle* sat on the ground beside the slipway, and Frankie and I sat inside it, with the workmen, drinking tea, and feeling properly grown-up. But my special pleasure was to go on board the newly arrived deep sea cargo ships as they unloaded timber, or grain or general cargo onto the jetties or into the nearby sheds.

The whole atmosphere of seagoing filled me with so much pleasure that I would gladly have sailed away at a minute's notice in any of those tramp steamers without giving my family a moment's thought. When I was only twelve I had already collected notes from four different ship's officers recommending me as a deck boy, and when the last remaining four-masted sailing ships called into Belfast to load cargo for Australia I was nearly mad with excitement.

A lady art teacher at the school I attended became

engaged to the second mate of one of those sailing ships. I used to follow her around with my eyes in school until she was driven to ask me why I kept staring at her? "Could you get me a job going to sea?" I asked. "If it'll stop you staring at me in that daft way," she said, "I'll do anything." That only made me worse. I used to wait for her to get off the bus near school every morning and ask her if there was any word yet. Eventually she pleaded to know what I would take to leave her in peace. "I'm beginning to get nightmares about you," she said. "When I come down to breakfast in the mornings, I'm half expecting to find you sitting eating toast, and asking with your mouth full if there's any word yet."

Well, I was always one to face up to the truth. "OK," I said, "I can see you're not interested in putting me to sea. Give me a shilling and that'll be the end of it." She gave me one and six, with a sigh of relief. The sailing ship concerned went aground off Cornwall later. I remember thinking that if that teacher had got me a job on it, it wouldn't have happened.

The truth of the matter is, I never did get away to sea. Without telling me, my father and mother were hoping that I would be the first McAughtry to get a white collar job. But I wasn't to know that in 1935.

The Blue Boat

Francis Harvey

How do I know that the wrecked blue boat
asleep in the long grass under the alder
dreams it is whole again and still afloat?

Because when I passed it by one night last week
and the wind made a sudden stir in
the trees I heard the sound of timbers creak
and the swish of a keel in the lake.

Holy Water and the German Bomb

Joe O'Donnell

I was seven years old, about to make my First Communion, and I hadn't a clue what an atheist was. For a long time I had heard that Mr. Nagle, our downstairs neighbour, was an atheist.

Adults said it softly, with a nod of the head. My mother pursed her lips when she said it, wiping out in one savage look, the man's - up to then - good character.

So when the Germans bombed Dublin in 1941, my mother laid the blame, fair and square, on Mr. Nagle.

"I knew we wouldn't have an hour's luck," she said.

There were three flats in our house, and my father, an NCO in the LDF, led all the families to the basement.

We knew the drill from school. You went to the lowest part of the house and lay down with your head between your knees, a safe if uncomfortable position.

There we all were in the basement, all three families listening to the rumble of the coming planes. The house, I have to say, was in Fairview, Dublin and not very far from the North Strand.

"She's headin' this way," said my father. That was when the second bomb fell. This time the whistle and bang were close.

My mother scrambled to her feet clutching the large bottle of holy water my aunt Eileen had brought back from her trip to Lourdes.

Holding the bottle in her hand my mother started to scatter all and sundry with the holy water.

"Sacred heart of Jesus, protect and defend us all. Sacred heart of Jesus, protect and defend us all."

The droning of the aircraft got louder, and my mother had to raise her voice above the noise.

"Sacred heart of Jesus, protect and defend us all."

Nagle turned a startled face towards her.

"Missus," he said in a tight, cracked voice, "Missus, don't come near me with that stuff. Do you hear me now?"

My mother, much as she disliked his beliefs or lack of them was ready to give the devil his due with death a mere bomb away.

"Don't worry, Mr. Nagle. I think it's more than a drop of holy water you need now," she said and carried on with the holy water.

Her aim was true, as like a knife thrower in a circus she rained either side of the stunned Mr. Nagle, without once wetting him.

It was at that very moment that the German plane chose to ditch its last bomb.

The whistle of this bomb was much louder than any of the other ones. And the bang when it came was much bigger and nearer than the others. It shook the house. A window broke with a crash upstairs. Dust rained down on us.

My mother yelled, "Jesus, Mary and Joseph!" and leaped back in fright. She fell over my father, and the bottle of holy water sailed through the air and smashed above the head of Nagle.

With a howl he leapt to his feet as though he had been scalded with boiling water.

"I'm wet, Missus. You've soaked me with that stuff."

We all looked at him in fear as he took off up the stairs. He didn't know what was happening outside. He didn't care. But whatever it was, it was safer than being soaked with Lourdes water inside.

Mr. Nagle never did forgive my mother for what took place the night of the bombing.

"Nothing will convince me," she said, "but that that was the devil you saw rushing out. Just as Jesus sent those pigs in the Bible running into the sea, that's what Aunt Eileen's holy water did to him. Mark my words, it wouldn't surprise me if we were to see a change of heart in the same Mr. Nagle."

It would make a neat ending if I could tell you that Mr. Nagle had a change of heart. Alas I can't. Mr. Nagle stayed firmly an atheist and died many years later, drowning off Curly's Hole in Dollymount.

My Neighbour

Morgan Llywelyn

That old man, twisted and bowed by his years,
Reminds me of an apple tree
That grew by my window long ago.

An apple tree twisted and bowed by its years
But spring's warm sun made it blossom
And crown itself with beauty.

So my neighbour's face
Comes alive again
In the warmth of a friendly smile.

Have You Forgotten?

Kathleen Kierse

Have you forgotten?
All grey winter long I was your friend.
Icy mornings I tracked across frosted grass
To put food on your table
And numb fingers made ready your bath,
Slave to your charms that I was.

Have you forgotten
The brown nuts I chose for your delectation
And the net bag of creamy suet
That kept your blood warm
And your feathers sleek?

Slave to your charms that I was,
A handy husband was cajoled
A roof rose over your table
To ward off the thieving magpies
A weighted base thwarted marauding dogs.
Have you forgotten?

You do remember, don't you,
How sweet the buds were on the plum trees
When harsh winter passed
And how you thumbed your beak at me

While I watched you strip them bare,
Mean little sod that you are.

Ah, you do remember!
A tell-tale blush stains your throat.
But you know darn well
That I'll forget your perfidy
And feed you again, when North winds blow,
Slave to your charms that I am.

Washing Up and Black Puddings

Eithne Strong

This night there was a new thing about the tea wash-up. Minnie put a tin tray on the table when all the crockery was shoved to the middle for washing. Kitty had seen the tray being bought that day in the hardware. They had all been in Ballyowen and Eily, the cousin on holidays from working in big English houses, was with them. It was a church feast day which meant no school but the Ballyowen shops opened all the same. Sheamus, who would have much preferred to stay at home, drove them in the pony-trap, resigned as usual to these town trips he had to make for the sake of family.

Kitty always wanted to know the why and wherefore of everything and she had questioned about the tray when they were in the hardware shop, only Minnie had shut her up with a low yet fierce, "Conduct yourself."

It was enough in front of people not part of the family. At home, Kitty would have gone on pestering with questions until tempers were lost.

Now, when Minnie put the tray down on the table, Kitty asked, "What's that for?"

Minnie pretended to be surprised. She said in a prim surprised way, "For the washing-up of course."

Kitty knew she said "of course" because Eily was there. For some reason her mother wanted the cousin to think the tray was the most usual thing in the world. But Kitty was at home now and not to be satisfied with a want of information. She spoilt things for her mother by going on, "but we have never had a tray for the wash-up before. What will you do with it?"

Eily was the one to answer. "It's to put the wet crockery on it," she said.

"What for?" Kitty went on .

"To collect the water," said Eily.

"Of course," Minnie said. The most usual thing in the world. Of course.

"But the water always dripped onto the floor before," Kitty kept on.

Red began to show on the sides and front of Minnie's neck.

"Well it did," Kitty insisted in spite of the red warning which she knew very well. "I never saw a wash-up but there was a pool of water on the floor after it."

"None of your cheek! Silence!" Censorship. Minnie used censorship when she was not sure of control. All her neck and the tops of her cheeks were red now, her upper lip stretched straight, a sign of severe strain. She was tired and finding it very hard to hold her temper. It would be a great relief to give Kitty a few sound wallops and a rattle of abuse but she was not going to do that in front of Eily. If it had not been for Eily the whole matter would never have come up anyway. For all Minnie had wanted was to show Eily that things in her house were not too backward compared with the way they were done in big houses in England. Her little plan with the tray, had it succeeded, would have been a tiny triumph, a small inner comfort.

She continued trying to make it succeed by ignoring Kitty, by acting as if she did not exist and therefore could not have spoken. Kitty certainly felt hurt by this, felt punished. She also hated Minnie for it. She had only spoken the truth but her mother would never admit that. Often her mother came to the point of believing her own little pretences because they mattered so much to her. If this question of the tray and the wash-up arose later between herself and Kitty, her mother by that time would be, very likely, quite convinced that she herself was entirely right.

Joe was watching and listening. No sympathy for his sister though. He was already making faces at her to show his pleasure in her defeat, even making mocking small noises from his corner. She pretended not to notice but he knew she saw and heard. She found it bitter that he was always glad if things went wrong for her, that he never ever showed a single sign of affection.

Yet *she* could feel pity for *him*. There was the night he was whipped because of the damage to the new wall-clock from Tralee. He was accused of cracking the glass and the fact that he denied doing it, again and again, was no use at all. Sheamus warned if he did not own up he would be whipped; the father of the family very much wanted his children to be truthful. And whipped Joe was. Kitty was greatly upset to see it. There he was, his trousers down, crying, denying. His naked thin white legs, awkward looking under the shirt tail, filled her with pity. Although often before she had been glad to see him punished, this was too shameful and she could feel no gladness in it. Even if he *had* broken the glass and, at the time, she thought he probably had. Later, many years later, when they were at last past the jealousies of childhood and could speak as two people who cared about each other, he told her that he had not. He told her calmly as if the wound to his spirit had been healed in the passing of the years. They both then began to think that Nelly might have been the culprit, that she accused him to Sheamus to escape blame herself. They agreed that was the kind of thing Nelly would do. By then, they had all gone away from the old homestead.

Nelly was about tonight but she had not seen the business with the tray. The air in the kitchen would not have been any pleasanter for Kitty had she been there. Nor would Nelly have been on Minnie's side either. She would have enjoyed seeing that the bare truth from Kitty had so flustered Minnie. She would have laughed her loud laugh, much like the sound a turkey made, and that laugh would have been at Minnie for trying to put on airs and at Kitty for getting the rough edge of her mother's tongue. No-one could depend on kind treatment from Nelly.

Soon she came in from where she had been trucking around outside with milk buckets. She sometimes did more of this than was needed, hoping while she was in Thady's way to start some spark out of him. But not much chance, no give at all in Thady. Anyway, Nelly did not get men easily. Not that she was short of looks, but men shied away from her bossiness which was often on the borders of a kind of hysteria. And what did that come from? Maybe it sprang from the secret blood of "Old Walrus" as Sheamus sometimes called Nelly's father when she was not there to hear.

Kitty could not remember a time when Nelly had not been a part of the household. She made periodic visits to her own family on the other side of the parish and a few times she had taken Kitty in the donkey-cart. Old Walrus had glowered from the corner of the hearth. He never said a word but every now and again he spat with venom, slicing the glowing turf. A long moustache drooled wetly down the sides of his bitter mouth. His wife was a worn version of Nelly but she had no bossiness in her face. Her eyes were unhappy. It was not a welcoming house. Evil hung there.

"He has driven in the cows for the fair in the morning," Nelly said. She was talking about Thady, the man who worked on the farm.

"Did he shut the two gates?" Minnie asked.

"Ah, don't you know he shut the gates," Sheamus said this with some impatience. He straightened out the newspaper; the pages of it shook a little all the time he held them. Joe and Kitty had often noticed this slight shake of his. Sometimes they felt sorry for him and other times they did not. There were times also when he was a butt for their mockery, open or secret, as they felt they could dare. Minnie openly made little of him but she did not go along with their doing it. Maybe because that held up a mirror to herself.

While the scene about the tray had been going on, Sheamus had been sitting in his usual nightly place and that was in the armchair with the sugawn bottom. It was huge and it was definitely his. He used to tilt its back legs and put his feet up on the bricks that made an arch above the range. He kept the paper at an angle for reading, over his knees. In this position he was safe for the time being from family tangles. He would hold his ground as long as possible and take no notice of most goings-on. But the remark about the cattle had caught his ear for the cattle were important to him. They were to be sold with profit, he hoped, the next day.

He said now, "He would have to be an awful gom to leave the gates open." But there was a grain of doubt in the way he said it. Maybe he should go himself to check on Thady. Only he was comfortable at last after the long drive in the pony-trap from Ballyowen. He did not want to stir again.

"Well, isn't he that, too, a gom?" The words from Minnie came in a very sharp tone. "Don't you know you can't depend on him. You have no choice but to see for yourself."

Sheamus was not a cursing man, not inside the family at any rate; now, he clacked his tongue several times, maybe ten times. Then he lowered his feet from their comfortable height and pushed back the legs of the heavy chair with a horrible grating noise on the flagstones. At the sound, Minnie closed her eyes for a long instant but she said nothing. To say something would mean to use more energy and she was weary, fit to drop. With a most unpleasant force, Sheamus cleared his throat of tobacco phlegm from many channels, not seeing the dislike of the sound in the faces around him. Without stooping his fine height, he lifted the kettle off the range and, through the round opening under it, spat into the fire. Perfect aim. A hiss came from the madly boiling spit and he watched it, a shrinking small ball, dancing itself out on a fiery sod. He put the kettle back and shuffled off his old slippers to pull on a pair of boots. Then out the back door he went.

"Joe and Kitty, time for you to be going to bed." Minnie had decided to notice Kitty's presence again.

"I won't go the same time as her," Joe said, brazen.

"You will go when you are told. Same time as *she* - mind your grammar."

"Whoever gets off shoes the first can stay longer?" Joe was in hope. Minnie made no reply. Oh, if only they would now go to bed without argument, without the need for discipline: that took so much energy.

"Whoever gets off shoes the first can stay longer?" Joe tried again.

"That's not fair," Kitty objected. "I'm made to wear boots and you'll have your shoes off the quickest."

She always had to wear boots because of her chilblains and the bad weather on the wet rough roads. Neither of them had made the smallest move yet to take off boot or shoe.

"Mam," Joe started off again, "the one that..."

"Oh, for God's sake," Nelly jabbed fiercely, "Missus, they are delirious with sleep - they should be in bed long ago."

"Ah, mind your own business, you shut up," Kitty snapped at her.

"How dare you!" This came like a razor from Minnie. It was supposed to seem a scolding because of the rudeness to Nelly but really it was because of Kitty's earlier attitude about the tray. "Both of you, not another tittle out of you. Conduct yourselves. No impertinence. To bed the two of you. At once."

Kitty went to kiss her mother. This she did every night, row or no row. Minnie stooped to meet her with an unrelaxed face. She was never humble with the children. Joe went upstairs. Kitty went to the room near the kitchen where her parents slept; her own room over the kitchen was given to Eily for the time being.

In her parents' room she twisted restlessly in the narrow bed against the dividing wall. The only light was from a Sacred Heart lamp, a very small one that made queer shadows everywhere. Sheamus's old pipes on a fretwork rack turned into shadows of demons. The big picture of John the Baptist and Jesus playing in a wood was no comfort at all to her. They were saintly, sinless children who had nothing in common with someone like herself.

In the kitchen, men had gradually gathered. A few of them had empty sacks across their shoulders tied, by strings from the top corners, across their chests. Not at ease with Minnie, they were more inclined than usual to shelter under their headgear although two took off their battered hats and hung them on their knees. Sheamus, back from the yard, stood taller than any of them. He had a natural dignity of appearance with his fine head and its heavy crop of white hair. The collar and tie he wore and the second best suit, these also made a difference between him and the men.

They were to take his cattle to the fair tomorrow when they took their own. A few matters had to be talked about. Minnie was sitting under the hanging lamp, mending a trousers of Joe's as fast as she could. She wanted to get to bed as soon as possible out of the men's way. She had good features but her face was set, severe, because she was tired and tense. The moment she was ready, she put the trousers over the back of a chair.

"Goodnight to you, men. I'll leave you all to your own affairs now."

Nelly and Eily had already gone upstairs. Minnie went into her bedroom and began to undress. After she had closed the door, there was a mumble of men's voices from the kitchen as well as an odd clear word. Kitty pretended to be asleep. She could hear her father's voice and some of what he was saying as he told the men what he wanted them to do about the cattle on the next day. The price of cattle, the way men traded in them, these things meant nothing to Kitty except the small break in the daily household habits they brought about, such as tonight. She heard her father, his voice suddenly very loud and strong. "Just so, just so."

Saying the thing twice, three times or more, his voice getting louder all the time, that was his way to make a point among people with whom he was at ease. But Minnie was always ready to check him. Even now, she put her head through the bedroom door to order in a snapping whisper, "Stop shouting, Sheamus."

Only he was too taken up to hear her. He was making his point to the men: "... and always keep a civil tongue ..."

"Sheamus, Sheamus," Minnie hissed a blistering whisper.

He turned towards the bedroom door, not sure what was wrong but feeling that in some way he was, once again, not pleasing Minnie.

"Haaa?" he shouted flatly. "Did you say something, Minnie?" She turned instantly furious. So often she was furious with him. But now, because of the men, she did not break into open abuse. But the way she spoke was like the hissing of an angry gander.

"Stop shouting, Sheamus! For God's sake, stop shouting. The children are asleep. Can't you conduct yourself!"

In the kitchen, all at once, there was total silence. Minnie jerked her head back into the bedroom. She knelt down by the big iron bed to say her prayers.

Kitty lay there wondering about her mother, why she was always so easily angry, why so snappy with her father, giving him no ground. A broad big man, twice the size of his wife. She was hungry for her mother to show more love. She wished her mother's words would not lash so fiercely at sensitive places. If only her mother would give her a cuddle sometimes, lift her up, even stroke her hair. Anything that would show she understood her troubled, fighting, frightened daughter. Why, instead, did she always seem impatient at signs of Kitty needing her? The child ached emptily.

Minnie, at last between the sheets, gave a long broken sigh and kept her still-tense hand bunched over the rosary beads under her pillow.

In her mind's eye, Kitty could see that in the kitchen her father would droop his great head and a blankness would settle over his face. Her mother often had this effect on him.

And, indeed, it was true that Sheamus had lost the

thread of what he was saying to the men. The two youngest had been his pupils in the small school. A few others were his own cousins from down the fields, less fortunate than he in opportunity and education. But all gathered in the kitchen understood the position about Minnie. They would put his mind at ease as to what was to be done.

"It is alright, master, we know what you were telling us. To keep a civil tongue in our heads, that was what you were saying. And that is what we will surely do. Leave it to us, it is good advice."

"All right so, men. Goodnight now, goodnight."

Depending on how well they knew him they said:

"Goodnight sir."

"Goodnight master."

"Goodnight Sheamus."

The spirit had sunk in him. He was relieved to be finished. He left them and came into the room and began getting ready for bed.

The men sat around in the warm kitchen. There they would stay until breakfast. They might or might not fall asleep. Kitty was still very much awake, although now lying quite still. She was picturing the men sitting around the range, waiting for a black morning start. She longed to be out there with them until the alarm clock got Nelly up. Nelly would come down to cook a hefty breakfast of pork steak and black puddings from the pig-killing yesterday at Pat Mick's, over across the rae.

She dozed and woke to hear the clang of iron fry pans on the range.

Nelly was up and putting to cook the pork steaks, the well-filled puddings with their stuffing of pinhead oatmeal, blood and onions.

A few of the men had fallen asleep in odd positions

and Nelly prodded them awake with the poker.

"Now boys, fine morning to you."

She pushed the kettle towards one of them. "Here, Mickeen, go down to the buckets and fill up the kettle from the spring water one. Make sure it is the spring you are filling with and don't be poisoning us with the water off the roof."

"Yerra, fill it yourself," said Mickeen, "that is what you are here for. You are here this morning to make us our breakfast. Well, go on and make it. We have our day's hardship before us."

Nelly knew she was out of luck and went herself to fill the kettle.

"A dying man would not have much hope of anyone here getting the priest for him," she yelled at him over the splashing.

But Mickeen was pleased with himself. "Dying man?" he said. "Strapping woman it is. Fine pair of collops." He prodded her legs with a long stick specially cut for the fair, and Nelly liked it. The nearness of all these men was stimulating. She flirted, shrill:

"Damn you. Were you saying hardship? Not much hardship for the likes of you. Blackguarding and boozing, more like."

In the bedroom Kitty could smell the black pudding cooking. What a great feeling to have breakfast while it was still pitch dark outside. But if she did venture out there to the kitchen, no one would want her. Even the cousins from down the fields would not want her and it was out of the question for her to know the delight of this breakfast, cooked over the roaring range while it was night dark outside the kitchen window. She knew very well Nelly wanted the men all to herself with Minnie out of the way, for once.

26

A horrible loneliness of being so young filled Kitty. A loneliness of being so separate from the marvellous world of the grown-ups with their special talk that was often hard to understand but was full of meaning for them; she was separate from them, with their mixed reasons for things, their secret kinds of understanding and jokes over her head, their brutal desirable laughter.

Minnie and Sheamus were asleep. She was in miserable isolation.

Becoming A Citizen

Philip Casey

My neighbour's children
are marshalled to the breakfast table,
hair brushed from the scalp out, en route.
They nibble on burnt toast smeared with jam,
their mother's voice just audible
over incessant radio music.

Of course they know all the lyrics,
miming and gyrating on a screen
in their sleepy brains.
As usual they're late.
They never seem to care
and ignore their haggard mother

who must push and pull
against the demon clock.
Their father is still in bed,
or gone to work,
or gone for good.
It's hard to know, sometimes.

All Wet Days

Alice Taylor

All her days were wet ones
And all her thoughts were sad.
And anytime you met her
You would regret you had.
She'd depress you drip by drip
And leave you feeling low.
She is a wet day woman
And will be always so.

A Daughter's Duty

Emma Cooke

"Your mother shouldn't dream of going home until well after the wedding, Eva. She should stay here with you until she's on her feet again," said Auntie Pat. Auntie Pat loved poking her nose into other people's business.

Eva kept a grip on herself. Her mother would have to make up her own mind about what she wanted to do.

"Oh Pat. I'm so much, much better. Why I'm as fit as a fiddle," Mrs. Kenny said in a thin weak voice.

Auntie Pat was not going to keep quiet. "Nonsense. Eva is just going to have to talk you out of it. You're not as well as you think you are, May. Eva wants you here. You gave us all a terrible fright. Besides..." she leaned forward, "What have you got to go home to? Nothing."

At this Mrs. Kenny, sitting in her son-in-law's own special armchair, collapsed back against its red back and Eva said, "Do stay, Mother, if you want to."

Her mother's pleased face reminded Eva of when she was a little girl and picked bunches of wild flowers for her as a birthday surprise. But she knew that Liam was going to be annoyed when he found out that Mother would be staying on.

Auntie Pat smiled at both of them. "There," she said, "I knew it was all nonsense about May coming home this weekend. I needn't have driven down to collect her after all."

I hate Auntie Pat, thought Eva. And Auntie Pat would have left by the time Liam got home so she was the one who would have to listen to Liam's complaints.

She knew exactly what it would be like. Liam would say: "You mean your Auntie actually drove down to collect your mother and then went home leaving her behind? That's the best I ever heard." Eva wished that Mother, just once, could be a fly on the wall in their bedroom listening to how grumpy Liam could be. Then perhaps she'd come to visit less often, and if she did happen to catch a bad dose of the flu she'd stay in at home in her own bed instead of arriving down here to be sick.

Liam was cross when he came home. "Your mother is a witch," he said. "And she doesn't like me."

"She's been sick, Liam," said Eva. She hated fighting.

"If that's the case she should be in hospital, not sitting in my house. And why does she sit in the only chair that I find comfortable?" Liam stuck out his chin the way he always did when he was in a bad humour.

"I told her to sit in your chair," Eva said, but she was too tired and miserable to go on.

"What does she do squatting there for hours? Hatch out turkey eggs?" Liam was going to stay furious.

"She'll be coming up with us in a week's time for Mary's wedding. She'll definitely stay on in her own place then," Eva said.

"She'd better." Liam stamped out of the kitchen and fifteen minutes later, when Eva went upstairs, she found him lying on their bed with his face to the wall. When she spoke to him he didn't answer. She hated the way that he could make things seem as if they were her fault. She hated it when he made himself out to be a martyr. She was the person who had to do all the extra work while Mother was here. When Liam behaved like this she was sorry that she had ever married him.

She wished that she was still single. Then when she was exhausted she'd be able to relax and do exactly whatever she felt like doing. And if Mother wanted to visit she could come for months at a time. The only trouble was that she was expecting a baby. It was still a secret between herself and Liam, she hadn't told her mother yet. She didn't feel like telling anyone right now when Liam was in such a bad mood.

"What's this?" Liam asked at suppertime, poking his fork through the sauce Eva had made as if he didn't like it.

It was a special fish sauce. It had taken ages to prepare and it had cost the earth.

"A boiled egg or a slice of ham and a tomato is all I need, Eva," said Mrs. Kenny and she shivered. "It's just, dear, sometimes your cooking is so rich..." her voice trailed away. She had barely touched her food.

Tears pricked at the back of Eva's eyes as she said, "Go into the sitting room, Mother, and sit by the fire. I can bring some tea and toast in a little while."

"I'm afraid I'm full up." Mrs. Kenny tried to laugh.

Eva felt worried as she saw how her mother gave a little stagger before walking away from the table. She hoped that Auntie Pat was wrong and that Mother could keep on living on her own. It was something she would have to try and sort out when they went up for Mary's wedding. She'd much rather talk to Mary about it than to Auntie Pat. Auntie Pat didn't want to be bothered about Mother. All she wanted to do was go off and play golf and cards with her friends.

Mary said that Mother cramped Auntie Pat's style. It was fine while Mary, who was Eva's cousin, was living nearby and could visit them both. But the trouble was that after the wedding she and her husband were going to go and live in Canada.

"Pat is beginning to grow down. Soon she'll be as small as I am. Have you noticed that, Eva?" Mother said later when she and Eva were sitting quietly by the fire. Liam had gone down to the local pub.

Eva shook her head. She had been wondering if this was a good moment to tell her mother that she was pregnant. Auntie Pat had looked the same as always to her. She sure hoped the baby didn't inherit Auntie Pat's beaky nose.

"Eva, I have to tell you that Dr. Moloney doesn't think I should be on my own." Her mother's voice suddenly got very shaky. "That's just his opinion, of course. I don't want you to think you have to do anything. I don't have to take it seriously." Her mouth looked like a squashed rosebud. Then she managed to say, "The nuns have quite a nice place - a home - outside the town." She had a scared look in her eyes which were the same dark brown as Eva's.

"I must tell you, Mother, I'm going to have a baby," Eva said in a rush. It wasn't at all the way she had intended to break the news. She had wanted it to be something very special. Instead it was all awkward and mixed-up.

"What's the face on about this time?" Liam asked as they got ready for bed. He had come home from the pub in better humour.

Eva didn't answer, but busied herself smoothing cream on her face.

"Cheer up." Liam gave the bottom of her black nightie a friendly pat. He had met some pals in the pub. He'd heard a good piece of business news. Eva's old mother had been tucked up in her bed by the time he got home. He grinned thinking of a mother-in-law joke one of his drinking pals had made.

"Are you alright, sweetheart?" He thought of how much he loved Eva. He had been a bit hard on her lately. Life shouldn't be all gloom. But he was only trying to help. If he didn't the old lady and that awful Auntie Pat would take over Eva's life - and his. Eva must look out for herself, especially now that there was, at long last, a baby on the way. They had been trying to have one for ages. Now the doctor said that they'd probably end up having five or six. Liam didn't mind how many they had. But he didn't want Eva's mother stuck here all the time, spoiling everything.

Eva finished cleaning her face and said, "Liam, Mother says that she can't live on her own. The doctor says she isn't well."

"But all she had was a dose of the flu, and your Auntie Pat is egging her on to make a fuss about it," shouted Liam. He wanted to say something even rougher. He'd go mad if Mrs. Kenny moved in on them. Eva would have to get used to the fact.

He ranted on while Eva just sat on the side of the bed staring at the pillowcases.

Then he took a deep breath and told the dirty mother-in-law joke that he'd heard in the pub. His heart grew heavy with rage. If Eva really brought her mother down to live here it meant that she wanted to kill him.

"You don't give a damn about me," he said. "Not a

tuppenny damn."

And to make things worse the sweet hollow at the nape of Eva's neck and the curve of her breasts under that crazy black nightdress was filling him with tormented longings. They were husband and wife for heaven's sake! He hadn't been near her for a fortnight. If she'd any feelings for him she'd know how he felt. He grabbed her without warning and pulled her towards his side of the bed.

He hadn't even time to get her nightdress off. Afterwards he held her head tight against his chest and rubbed his chin against her brown curls. He didn't care anymore about what happened to Mrs. Kenny. No matter what she tried he'd be able for her.

Sometime later Eva slipped out of bed and padded quietly down to the bathroom. She was afraid to run the shower in case it disturbed Liam or her mother. Instead she sponged herself from neck to toe with a big yellow sponge. Then she stuffed the black nightie into the laundry basket and put on the blue cotton pyjamas Auntie Pat had given her for Christmas. They made her feel a little better. Liam hated her in these pyjamas. The fact made her feel more comfortable. She wondered if she had really fallen out of love with him or if the mood would pass. She had been lying for an hour or so staring through the darkness at where the back of his head was and thinking how his skull would crack open if it was hit hard by the wooden base of the bedside lamp.

She was four months pregnant. She needed cherishing. She sat down on a little round stool. She didn't have the energy to take on Liam and her mother at the same time. If Liam ever left her she'd have no means of support. She didn't know how she was going to get through the coming months.

She sat very still on the little stool waiting - waiting for inspiration. Next spring she was going to be a mother herself, she was going to be very busy. For the child's sake she must learn to be strong. But somehow just thinking of the baby made her feel as if a sweet red jelly was dissolving at her very centre. When she thought of the baby she couldn't hate anybody, especially not Liam even if he had pressed himself on her when she was so weary and worried.

"You're all I have, Eva." Her mother's voice echoed in her head. "I don't want to upset your life. I'm just letting you know what the doctor says." She couldn't spurn her mother.

And there was no point in asking Auntie Pat to help. Auntie Pat had been trying to get Mother out of the way since the year dot. Oh - what was she to do? Nothing, nothing at all except keep her fingers crossed and wait until after she had seen Mary married.

She hoped Mary was going to be happy. She hoped Mary wasn't making a big mistake. She hoped the baby was going to be a girl then, when she herself was old and ill, she'd have somebody to mind her. "You'll have to stand up to them," Liam said as if it was the easiest thing in the world.

When she stood up her knees were inclined to buckle. She had been looking forward to the future, now she felt that it was going to be dreadful.

She made a face at the tin of powder for her mother's dentures standing on the window-sill. Six months ago she'd had a chance of taking a lover. Another man had asked her to leave Liam and come away with him. She had refused. Her pregnancy, when she had almost given up hope of having a baby, had seemed like a reward. Oh, if only she had been able to see ahead! She held onto the sill and stared through the clear glass on the top window-pane. The sky was coal black and she felt very small and helpless. Smaller than the smallest star.

Lifelines

(for Niamh)
Michael Coady

Daughter, your eyes
are clearer than mine:

you've asked me why the top
and bottom of my pint don't mix

and why we're dropping coins
into a model lifeboat.

I've said that heavy things
sink to the bottom, and there are

unexpected storms, lives to be
snatched out of the wind.

Later in the rain
you take my hand

lead me through
a tumult of dark trees.

I flare a match
and fumble with the key.

Your face and hair are wet,
your eyes are shining.

Writing
Anne Le Marquand Hartigan

I am writing poems
on a May morning
on the back of my son's drawings.

Or is it that he has drawn pictures
on the back of my scribbles?

Anyway, my words are warmer
for his backing.

Ping Pong

Harry Barton

My son, Olaf, had his eighth birthday in 1960 when we were living in Sussex. We gave him the largest present he'd ever had, and, as it turned out, the best we'd ever given him. There was later a problem to do with handicapping in games, but you can't have everything.

"It's very big," Olaf said, as he began to open it.

"It's four feet long by two feet wide," I said.

"It's a table. It's a table-tennis table."

"That's right," I said. "Ping pong."

"It's a very small table," he said.

"This is a very small house," his mother said.

"It's got no legs," he said.

"It's a table-top. We thought we'd sit it on the table in your room."

I carried it up to the first floor and then on up Olaf's personal staircase to his attic room with its dormer window. He followed me with the bats, the ball and the net.

The table-top fitted neatly onto the table. There was room for us at each end, though my head was threatened by the slope of the roof. We didn't even have to move the bed. We set up the net, each fastening an end. I opened the window. "You should open the window every morning," I said.

He picked up a bat. He was standing awkwardly at one end.

"I'll show you," I said. "Come close to the table. Hold the bat in front of your fat tummy."

"It's not fat."

"In front of your thin tummy. Like this. As though you were guarding it." I demonstrated. "Backhand, it's called. It's the first shot to learn. At least, I think so. Now, I'm going to hit it to you and you're to try and hit it back. Try to hit the ball just at the moment it hits the table on your side of the net. Just push at it."

I served a ball gently across the little board of a net. I felt gigantic.

Olaf prodded and missed.

I picked up the ball and served again. Olaf prodded.

The ball went out of the window.

"I hit it," he said, delighted. He ran to the window.

"Look," he called. "Mitty's got it."

"Cats love ping-pong balls," I said. "Better than life itself."

Olaf and I became adept. Every time we hit the ball we had to make it go over the little board and land on a two-foot square. But we learned to do it, and to do it with magical swiftness, from close up or from a far corner of the room. It was real table-tennis. It was the perfect game, the one a father could enjoy as much as his son, not just for the few weeks after a birthday, but for years and for ever.

Because I was forty-four and he was eight, I could always win. When he won it was because I had let him. All fathers have this skill at all games. I learned to hit the little net instead of getting the ball over it. I became able to hit the ball so that it missed the table, but only just. For distraction, I would do an air-shot and clown about my foolishness. All fathers are efficient cheats and liars.

One day, between games, I suggested handicapping. He asked why. I said I had always been enthusiastic about handicapping, whether in games or races. My enthusiasm, I said, began in 1929 when I was thirteen, and watched the Ulster Tourist Trophy motor race on the Ards Circuit in County Down. It was a fourteen-mile circuit and the big cars had to go round thirty times, over 400 miles in all, chasing after smaller cars with fewer laps to cover. The race went on all day. The cars were touring and sports cars of every make and size, sixty of them, crowding the road. They had leather straps round their bonnets, I said.

Olaf looked blank, but I was undeterred. I went on talking.

The road was narrow by today's standard. "The roads of Ulster," my mother said, when the white centre line was introduced, "are not wide enough to keep to one side of." But this did not bother the goggled drivers, rocketing past in cars with flimsy mudguards and spare wheels strapped to their sides. As each went past, I ticked it off. I had a clip-board. On it was a piece of school graph paper. Down the left-hand side were the makes and race numbers of the cars. Across the top, the laps were numbered, one to thirty. For cars with handicaps I had blacked out the laps they wouldn't have to do.

All day long I watched a large white Mercedes and a smaller Alfa Romeo chasing two Baby Austins up through the field. The German, Caracciola, in his Mercedes, started at scratch; the Italian, Campari, in the Alfa Romeo, had two laps start; and the little Austins had five whole laps to help them. At last, towards the end of the day, the Mercedes was in the same lap as the Austins. Overtake the little cars once more and it would be ahead in the race. I started up the road, waiting to see which would come round the corner first, white Mercedes or little Austin with wheels like bicycle wheels. It was the Mercedes, just ahead of the two Austins. The only other car to overtake them was Campari in his Alfa Romeo. First place, then, to Mercedes at scratch; second to Alfa Romeo, starting twenty-eight miles ahead; third and fourth to Austins, with their seventy long miles of start.

"I'll never forget that day," I said to Olaf. "I still have the piece of graph paper."

My son stood there in his red cotton shirt, bat in hand, thinking his own thoughts.

"I'll show it to you one day," I said.

He spoke. "Could we have another game?" he asked.

"Certainly," I said, "and we'll try handicapping."

My starting at minus-ten to his plus-ten made it a long game.

But I didn't care. I no longer had to dissimulate; I could play to win. All through the long game, I could concentrate, working my way steadily forward, cutting down the gap. I was the young Rudi Caracciola, driving hard all day, steadily reducing the lead of the Austins. I won, 21-17. I was proud of myself. We played again. This time, Olaf won, 21-18, another close game.

I congratulated him, heartily. He smiled politely. He appeared listless, even unhappy. For either of us to be unhappy at table-tennis was extraordinary.

We went down the two flights of stairs to supper. It was fish fingers. In those days fish fingers and tomato ketchup induced ecstasy in Olaf. But not that evening. He just ate them, that was all. For four days we didn't play. This was the longest gap in living memory, four whole evenings without the sound of ping pong in the little house.

On the fifth evening we started playing again. We didn't decide this out loud. We just went upstairs and played. We didn't have handicapping. We didn't decide about this either. We just didn't have it. We never had it again. It was sad for me but we never did.

In 1968, we went to the west of Ulster to live. We built a house for ourselves. My wife had spent two years designing it on sheets and sheets and sheets of paper. We had lived in sixteen different houses and she knew exactly what she didn't want and exactly what she did want. What we, the table-tennis players, wanted was a Ping Pong Room, and we got it. The architect showed it as a Storeroom but we knew better. A full-sized table-tennis table is nine feet long by five feet wide. We stipulated a Ping Pong Room fifteen feet long, giving a three-foot run-back at each end, not much, but adequate; we could hardly expect to have a stadium built into the house. The room was wide enough to hold a work-bench, a deep freeze, two cat beds, a vegetable seed propagator, a stack of bee-hive frames, and enough pot plants to start a rain forest.

Olaf was now sixteen, and we had the best matches we had ever had. We had the long fast rallies of players who know each other's game. We swung at the ball with complete confidence. However hard it came at us, we could return it. We were conjurers, exhilarated, sometimes astonished, by our competence. We scored with references to history, in the fashion familiar to table-tennis players: 18-5, Battle of Trafalgar; 18-15 Battle of Waterloo; 19-16, Battle of Jutland. We used the Chronicle of Events in Pears Cyclopaedia: 10-16, Canute to the Throne of England; 15-20, Field of the Cloth of Gold, change service. We were historians as well as conjurors.

I no longer yearned for handicapping. I found to my

delight that I had to play flat-out to win. Indeed I noticed that I did not always win. It seemed to work out about even. There were also games in which I seemed unable to do anything right; I would lose 21-8 (Man Reaches Mars) or some score equally disgraceful. But I wasn't a champion; I didn't have to be inexorably reliable as well as a genius.

Then one evening, Olaf asked the question. He was lying on his face, reaching behind the deep freeze for a lost ball. "I was wondering," he said, the diffidence in his voice muffled by the deep freeze. "I was wondering whether you would like a handicap."

I was stunned. Olaf recovered the ball, pushed himself backwards along the floor and got to his feet. Even now, I can see him standing there, a huge potted plant - a jade tree - behind his head with its heavy 1960's shock of hair.

"You used to be very keen on handicapping," he said. "You talked about a motor race you went to as a boy."

"The Ards Circuit T.T," I said. "Three successive years." I stared past him at the jade tree with its dozens of small fat jade-green leaves. "I don't think I want a handicap," I said. "I don't think so."

"O.K.," said Olaf. We went on with the game. There was a close finish. Anyone, I'd have thought, might have won.

When we stopped for the evening, I put my bat down on the table, trapping the ball under it. "Why don't I want to be given a handicap?" I asked.

Olaf put his bat down. "The drivers of the small cars in your motor race - "

"The Austin Sevens," I said.

"Whatever," said Olaf. "The drivers of those small cars knew they couldn't win without a handicap. When I was eight, I believed I could sometimes really win without a handicap. After all, three years before that, I had believed in Father Christmas."

"It's forty-nine years since I believed in Father Christmas," I said.

He smiled all over his face. "The principle's the same," he said.

Now, Olaf has long since left home, to travel and marry and become a father.

Last week they came on a visit and I watched my son let his son win. The boy is now twelve and plays very well; they have had the little old four-by-two table-top for years now. They even took it abroad with them. Olaf lied and cheated, his technique impeccable. He's caught between two generations: he has to let the boy won; he had to let me win. The score, as so often, was 21-19.

It was my turn to play the boy. "You'll need to watch out," Olaf told him. "This man would win any world championship for the over-seventies."

"I'll be careful," the boy said.

"Would you like a handicap?" I asked, without thinking.

"What for?" The boy was surprised.

We played. It was the greatest fun imaginable to have the old table out again. I began by being careful not to get ahead; I then found myself fighting to stay level, much less in the lead. It was a long game, going to twenty-all and four deuces. I won. I sat down on a stool, my bones aching a little. I was pleased with myself. "You were right," I told my grandson. "There was no need for handicapping." The boy didn't say anything. The three of us played the running-round-the-table game, hitting the ball and moving round the table and hitting it again, keeping it in play. The boy departed, shouting with laughter.

I sank back onto the stool. Olaf was watching me; it

was a kindly look, but knowing. I stared at him. Behind him, in the same earthenware pot, was a descendant of the old jade. "Are you trying to tell me," I asked, "that your horrible son let me win?"

"I didn't suggest it to him," Olaf said. "Someone must have told him to be kind to the aged."

"I never noticed," I said. "His technique must be excellent."

"It's hereditary," said Olaf.

I See You Dancing, Father

Brendan Kennelly

No sooner downstairs after the night's rest
And in the door
Than you started to dance a step
In the middle of the kitchen floor.

And as you danced
You whistled.
You made your own music
Always in tune with yourself.

Well, nearly always, anyway.
You're buried now
In Lislaughtin Abbey
And whenever I think of you

I go back beyond the old man
Mind and body broken
To find the unbroken man.
It is the moment before the dance begins,

Your lips are enjoying themselves
Whistling an air.
Whatever happens or cannot happen
In the time I have to spare
I see you dancing, father.

Diary
Desmond Egan

The thirtieth of a wet May
so different from last years!

hawthorn along the hills below Slane -
bluebell Celbridge - our supermarket of sun -
Killiney the colour of Smithwicks -
and the slow warm evenings dying into Leeson Street -

tonight at my bookcase
new rain was sneaking like weeks across glass
when I just happened to notice the stained diary
1973 inked on its spine put away
like an old book of poems in a leather binding

Summer

Val Mulkerns

Sarah's flight had not yet been called and there was plenty of time. Her baggage checked in, she was deep now in a fashion magazine, blue-jeaned knees together and feet spread wide. She looked carelessly uninvolved as though she were sitting on the floor of her untidy room.

"Have you your passport safely stowed away?"

"Oh, Mother, you saw me do it at the check-in."

"Did you actually take the Kwells? I last noticed them in your hand."

"I actually took the Kwells. Look, relax. I have my francs and my traveller's cheques and my separate embarkation fee. I have your presents for the Vendrons (whenever I see them) and twenty changes of socks. It's not my first flight and I haven't failed my entire exam, just Structures like everybody else. I won't jump out of the plane as we take off and I won't crunch up all the travel pills. I won't die of dysentery and I'm unlikely to fall into the hands of a really competent rapist. You should know by now I'm better able to take care of myself than you are and I'm delirious to be escaping. There, they're calling my flight. Number 8 gate."

With her magazine tucked into the big canvas shoulder-bag, she stood tall and smiling down at Emily, clean black hair falling around her narrow face, eyes already away and somewhere else. On the escalator she bent and laid her cheek, moist and cool as a fruit, against Emily's.

"There isn't anywhere in the world I'd rather be going. Your fault. You made me a lover of France before I left my pram. You taught me French nursery rhymes when you should have been teaching me ABC. You exchanged me for a Vendron child at the tender age of twelve and I've never been more terrified in my life than on that first plane flying off alone into the unknown."

"You were being met at the airport."

"Yes, but I didn't believe it. I didn't believe I'd live so long, and I wanted to howl like an infant and beg you to call it all off and let me live shamefully ever after."

"You looked so cool," Emily remembered. She had believed all the turmoil was inside herself. The forlornness of the school blazer. The smallness of Sarah as she had stumped across the tarmac, handgrip held in both arms like a puppy. Yet a few minutes previously she had kissed them coldly goodbye, exchanged a few giggling jokes with her friends who had stayed the night to be in time to see her off. That was all of eight years ago.

"Tell Denis when he gets back," she said carefully at the gate. "Tell him I said goodbye." At the age of three Sarah had called her mother Emily but had reverted soon afterwards to custom. Her father had always remained Denis. "Tell him thanks for the money and I'll write - well, sometime. Tell him, won't you?"

"I'll tell him. And I hope the job turns out to be interesting. I wouldn't mind being in your shoes myself."

"Why don't you come?" Eyes wide open in the hardworked pale face, Sarah really seemed to mean it.

"Don't be silly. Give the Vendrons my love - especially Nathalie."

"Of course, though I may not see much of them. Thanks for the lift, Mother, and the money and everything. And I will write - promise."

"Ask them over for Christmas if they'd like to come."

"Perhaps. But you know their position about the grandmother. Goodbye Mother."

"Goodbye, love. Bon voyage." They kissed briefly.

Due to the new security regulations you couldn't go any further, but by good fortune she caught sight of Sarah ten minutes afterwards, swinging long-legged across the tarmac, her baggy shirt about to take off by itself, it seemed, in the strong wind. Sarah was among the tallest of the hurrying passengers and there was about her an air of joyful freedom, from study, from Dublin, naturally from home. The small squat creature in the school blazer had gone bravely to her doom. In one sense she had never come back.

Denis had stood too and watched the plane take off that first time, a great menacing bird with flames at its tail. They had not admitted to feeling sick with worry, but Denis had taken her hand and squeezed it fiercely. She stood alone now on the balcony waiting for take off. The warm wind got inside her cotton dress, lifting it free, as she made her ritual wordless prayer for a safe arrival. Sarah was beyond her care now, a woman with the right to the wrong decisions so long as they were her own. She imagined the pale bony face tilted back in the seat, the capable bony hands fixing the seat belt, hands that could sketch, paint, make detailed plans for houses she might never build, cook, sew, and no doubt make love.

The plane was ready now. The crew had gone aboard

and now the pilot mounted the steps with a nod of thanks to the men who had fuelled his engines. Sarah was in the care of other people. For ever now. Emily watched the flames, saw the plane which had taxied toy-like around the runway shudder into flight and climb steeply into a grey June sky. She waved as Sarah was perhaps invisibly waving. Bon voyage.

Brown-stained fingers had pressed into her arm that first time. "She's beginning her independence. Already detached from us, already chatting to strangers on either side of her. She's safe and happy and being met at the airport. She doesn't even remember that we exist any more. Come and have a drink."

Shakily they had drunk without words to Sarah's safety, Sarah's happiness, Sarah's proficiency at French. The two friends with school blazers like Sarah's sucked their coke nervously through straws. They were a little lost now that Sarah was gone. At home in the suddenly empty house she and Denis had made urgent love before he went to work, one of the few completely spontaneous occasions she could remember. It had ended in laughter because the cat had been under the bed and squawked at the rustling springs before leaping out onto the window sill. Sunshine through the open window. The blinking black cat. A lawn-mower whirring somewhere. I love you.

On the way home from the airport she dropped in on friends who (she had forgotten) were away on holiday. She spent an hour at an exhibition in the National Gallery and had lunch there; a wandering afternoon in town followed. Twice she went into a public phone box and stood irresolute, the phone poised. When you didn't ring I thought perhaps you were ill again so I decided to check. How are you? No. It was over. She put back the receiver, preferring not to hear that cautious voice inventing the customary lies. It had been good and it was over and no harm done unless she made a fool of herself now. During a heavy shower she went into a cinema and stayed although she had seen the film before. It hadn't been worth anybody's time in the first place. She had another cup of coffee somewhere else and finally home could not be put off any longer. There was a letter on the kitchen table.

Emily, I'm unlikely to be back early. Hope Sarah went off OK and that she didn't forget anything vital. Thanks for the salmon I found in the fridge. I've somehow remembered to order a pint less milk for tomorrow but I could find no food for the cat. You should turn in early after all the rush of getting Sarah off. Try this Lionel Davidson - I liked it. D.

The note was under the paperback. It was half past eleven and still not quite dark in the garden. A warm breath of fading hawthorn came through the open window. She saw herself reflected in the glass, the note from Denis in one hand, his book in the other. This was the time Sarah would sometimes come running along the hall upstairs when she'd let herself in after the last bus. They would make coffee in the kitchen and turn over the news of the day. Jer and Catherine had broken it off again. Fergus had walked out on the parents and was sleeping rough in Stephen's Green. His old dear had recently started to open his letters and sniff around for drugs. She was too stupid to know that what she ought to be sniffing around for was bombs.

The old cat rubbed against Emily's ankles, bundled clumsily across the tiles to the empty bowl and back again to her ankles. Denis had been right - there was no cat food in the fridge. She had forgotten to get it at the butcher's yesterday. Maybe a saucer of milk would do. No. The furry collision with her ankles began all over again, a rasping of the tongue against her bare flesh, the clumsy journey back again to the milk-filled bowl. So far the creature was not howling; that would come later. Sighing, she fetched a slice of bacon from the fridge and cut it up with the kichen scissors but that too was rejected, so there was only one thing to do. Hurriedly she gathered into a saucepan a heap of unpicked chicken bones. Since they had been reserved for soup anyway there was nothing to lose by simmering them now instead of tomorrow and there was supper to gain for the cat who knew this routine and had now given up demanding instant food. It sat at her elbow as she opened the book, making its wheezy attempt at purring.

Tired of the sound, Emily wandered upstairs to run a bath. Idly stepping into Sarah's room while the bath filled, she saw herself once again reflected in the blank window above the dark garden and because she didn't like what she saw she quickly pulled across the curtains. The room smelled more than ever of Sarah, of youth. Yellow lamplight showed her the total disorder, maddening when Sarah was at home, childlike and touching now that she was gone.

Rejected garments for the suitcase overflowed from the open chest of drawers, littered the bed, joined a jumble on the floor of text books, sketch books, hair rollers, paper patterns, snippets of the new summer dresses she had made in the last few days, a half-eaten Mars bar and an unused tampon. The window seat was completely obscured by similar litter including shoes, boots and sandals as though they had been deliberately laid out the way a child lays out coloured sweets for selection. Compulsively Emily began to make order, interrupting the job once to turn off the bath water, then returning to sift, discard or rearrange the litter of Sarah's life.

'Soyez realiste,' she had written across the cover of a big sketch book, 'demandez l'impossible.' Not only did Sarah ask the impossible but sometimes she did it. It was during the week before one of her examinations that she had made a summer dress for Emily's birthday. No snippet of cotton had appeared anywhere to suggest what was to come, no piece of paper pattern had been left to give the game

away.   A blue cotton dress perfectly finished to the last
detail and a perfect fit had been dumped one morning into
her arms before Sarah banged the door and raced away to a
lecture for which she was already late.

Inside a college magazine called Structures there was
a sheet of paper that drifted free as Emily gathered all the
magazines together:

Arm-strapped together we watched up west
The blood of murdered day breaking night's rest.

Motorbikes.   The boy whose first effort this was used
to come surrounded by them as Aengus was by birds.   He
didn't own a motorbike but he collected friends who did.
That summer motorbikes crowded for ever on the bare patch
they had made under the trees.   Indoors Simon and
Garfunkel and the buzz of voices after school, Sarah's room
overflowing onto the stairs.   Coffee and 'Bridge Over
Troubled Waters'.   Shouts of laughter.   Always more boys
than girls.   The one who wrote the poem also fed the cat
while they were away on that last family holiday.   Because
he loved cats he had come in every day for a month and he
had sent on selected post also.   The house had not felt
empty when they came home.   He was a big brown curly
bear of a boy - what was his name? Ruairí.   He had left a
note with the month's bills on the kitchen table.

They all arrived too late to send on except 2 which were
filed in my impeccable system under W for 'Where do I put
these?' Céad míle fáilte (approx equal to 400 new fáiltes).
Cheers.   Ruairí.

The note fluttered out with the poem and the closing
fragment of a letter.   *But me no goodbyes.   Parting is such*
sweet whatyacallit.   Brightness falls into the lair.   Give you
good morrow.   Your sleepless step-in wolf.

He was dead two years now, found a tangle of bones
and burnt metal when he crashed a borrowed motorbike one

Saturday night on the Bray Road. These pages Sarah had kept together were evidently a memorial collection. *But me no goodbyes. Parting is such sweet whatyacallit.*

Sarah's sheets were rumpled but changing them would have seemed like rejection. They smelled of lemon soap and patchouli and made a warmer bed than the one upstairs. After a bath she was reading Sarah's Tolkien and half asleep when a key turned in the hall door. Switching off the light was instinctive but sleep was now far away. A smell of burnt bones crept up from the kitchen and already the heavy footsteps of Denis were sounding from that direction. He would find a starving beast and a ruin of spoiled supper. She began to laugh with hysterical guilt and then put her head under the clothes to stifle the sound. Faintly she could hear the yowls of the cat in panic-stricken welcome and her mind followed Denis's movements. First things first. He would switch off the cooker. Then open windows and doors wide. Then comfort the afflicted animal. Most probably he would make such a determined effort that he would find the cat something apart from the piece of uncooked salmon in the fridge. She had one impulse to go down and make abject apologies but in a little while this impulse was completely conquered. Tomorrow would be time enough.

She woke next morning to a silent house and sun flooding through the curtains. The house felt empty, which was impossible. Downstairs, nevertheless, it was empty, with a note on the kitchen table to prove it.

Emily, I'm afraid you forgot the chicken bones again. Cleared up as best I could and found a tin of cat food out in the car - dating from that camping holiday years ago, I have no doubt. It seemed quite fresh however and the cat didn't complain. You were sleeping so soundly I didn't like to waken you to let you know I must put in a few hours work to make up for a broken day yesterday when I had to see Henderson.

Appointment with the Minister on Monday morning and practically no background data prepared. May not get home for lunch so don't wait. D.

Working on Sundays was something new but then his partner was on holiday. If Denis could find the slightest excuse for extra work he wouldn't hesitate. She wanted to ring him and apologise, say something to hear him laugh. But there was nobody on the switchboard. Even if she drove into the main entrance the office block would be closed to everybody who hadn't a private key - he might as well be on the moon.

She opened the windows wide and hoped the reek of burnt bones would go away in the sunshine. Leaning out on the window sill she sniffed the morning. Hawthorn still, and wild garlic, and a hint of tom cats. In a moment there was the creak of a basket behind her and the huge woolly creature walked stiff-legged across the tiles. Its fur in the sunlight was a decayed brownish black, profuse because of remote Persian ancestry. Its golden goat's eyes avoided her when it lumbered up on the window sill. Nevertheless it sat companionably by her elbow and yawned, diffusing its old cat smell.

Mechanically she stroked it, and its strange rattling purr grew louder.

It was so old that it had curled up beside Sarah in the cot, guarding her from wasps in summer and from boredom at all times. Its name was Simpkin and Denis claimed that some vital mechanism (like the gizzard of a goose) had stopped working inside so that the cat had no way of dealing with the accumulation of fur swallowed when it washed itself. That is, it had one way, recently devised. Sometimes Emily would find a ball of fur and mucus near its basket on the tiles and for a few days it would sound less wheezy before the fur built up again. Eventually, she supposed, it would choke and then they could keep a dog instead.

It licked her wrist now with a rasping tongue before lumbering over the window sill into the garden. All old creatures, animal and human, move in the same way. Simpkin walking across the lawn looked more than somewhat like Aunt Harry. It was Sunday. "Just as soon as I pack Sarah off I'll be over to see you," she remembered saying. Sarah was wakening up in Paris or already sitting on the balcony, drinking café au lait out of a big bowl, apricot jam heaped into a split roll on her plate. There isn't anywhere in the world I'd rather be going, Sarah had said. But this was Dublin and today was Harry's day. Turning on her heel to make coffee, Emily found herself sliding on the tiles and bent down to see why. The ball of mucus and fur had been silently left at her feet, like an offering.

Cat
Kevin O'Connor

Prowling from the garden rear
Under branch-bowed trees you came
And found me here
Confronted me with narrow glint
Not a hint of fear or favour
Just your trenchant beauty ever
From wind and light and air outside
And threw my soul to liquid light
And knew you threw my soul to liquid light
Cat, I wonder what you're at..?

For Rita With Love.......
(Downs Syndrome)
Pat Ingoldsby

You came home from
your special school
in your special school bus
full of people
who look like you
and love like you
and you met me
for the first time
and you loved me.
You love everybody
so much so that it's
not safe to let
you out alone.

Eleven years of love
and trust and time
for you to learn
that you can't go on
loving like this.
Unless you are stopped
you will embrace every
person you see.

Normal people don't do that.
Some normal people will hurt you
very badly because you do.

Cripples don't look nice
but you embrace them.
You kissed a wino on the bus
and he broke down and cried
and he said, "Nobody has kissed me
for the last thirty years
but you did."
You touched my face
with your fingers and said,
"I like you."
The world will never
be ready for you.
Your way is right
and the world will
never be ready.

We could learn everything
that we need to know
by watching you
going to your special school
in your special bus
full of people
who look like you
and love like you

and it's not safe
to let you out alone.

If you're not normal
there is very little hope
for the rest of us.

The Landlady's Tale
Gerry O'Malley

A little sherry, dear? Go on, that's right. It'll do you good.

Oh, dear me, yes. I've seen all types. All kinds and types I've seen. Well, it's twenty years, dear...twenty years I've been running this house. Yes, it does seem a long time, doesn't it dear? Twenty years. Since Mr. Clarke passed away. Poor Mr. Clarke - ever such a nice man he was. Never a cross word between us, never a cross word. Which is more than I can say for my other two husbands. Ah...didn't know I'd been married three times, did you, dear? Well, I have. Mr. Clarke was my third. It was my second that left me the house. Mr. Ramsbottom. Left me independent, I'll say that for him. But he hadn't a warm disposition, Mr. Ramsbottom hadn't. If you know what I mean. And I never liked being called Mrs. Ramsbottom. Never could get used to it. To be quite honest, I used to feel a bit embarrassed. At the greengrocer's or the butcher's. Especially at the butcher's, dear. Still...it was nice to get the house.

Of course, the gossips said it was just for the house that Mr. Clarke married me. Well, they were wrong. It was True Love between Mr. Clarke and me. He was a few years younger than me, mind, but ailing. Very weak chest had Mr. Clarke. Poor Mr. Clarke.

The worst part of the winter had gone...1956 it was... when along came this cold snap at the end of March. You know what they say about March, dear? "In like a lamb and out like a lion." Funny, I don't remember how it came in that year, but it went out like a lion all right. And took poor Mr. Clarke with it. Chest. Buried him on the first of April. Yes, April Fools' Day, I remember that. Didn't seem right, somehow. Not dignified.

Well, up till then I'd had just one or two PGs (paying guests, dear) and the occasional B & B, but after Mr. Clarke passed away I went in for it properly. Well, I had to, my dear, didn't I? All the rooms done over, hot water everywhere, handbasins, a new bathroom...oh, the outlay! I moved down here to the lower regions myself. It's private. And my own entrance.

One thing I've always been most careful about and that is to keep a respectable house. An orderly house. Oh, I don't let to every Tom, Dick or Harry that knocks on the door. Rather leave a room vacant for a week I would. Until a suitable one came along.

Although, mind you, even the most experienced of us can make mistakes. There've been one or two I came to have my doubts about. And...not without reason, as things transpired.

Parties! Don't talk to me about parties! Well, you know, dear, I like a good "knees-up" myself as much as anyone. But I discourage the PGs. Disturbs the others, you know. And the neighbours. Gives the house a bad name. Oh, you can't be too careful.

Had to make a House Rule: No Parties. The young people were the worst. The music! My dear! More like a cat caught under a chair, if you ask me. I've stopped taking young PGs. Know what I mean "young"? Denim and guitars and that. Even university students. You'd think they'd be a better class. Well, I had my fill of them, I can tell you. Funny to think they're all qualified now...well, most of them anyway. Doctors, dentists, solicitors. Very respectable, I'm sure. Oh, very posh. I don't know how some of them...you know I honestly don't know how some of them found time to do any studying.

One young fellow was always bringing girls to his room. I had to speak to him. I told him, I said, "Mr. Hanley," I said, "it's against the Rules of the House to have ladies in your room after 10 o'clock." "Why is that, Mrs. Clarke?" he said. Oh, yes, straight out, bold as brass. "Well," I said, "well, Mr. Hanley, it doesn't look right. You'll find the same rule in any respectable house. And this is a respectable house, Mr. Hanley." That's what I told him. And do you know what he said to me? He said, "You don't have to worry about me bringing girls here, Mrs. Clarke," he said. "I'm a homosexual," he said. Well...I didn't know where to look. Fancy that! And an innocent expression on his face while he was saying it. Well, I gave him his marching orders, I can tell you. To say that to me...straight to my face...without so much as a blush! I mean...well...what would you have done? There are limits, after all. I'm as broad-minded as the next, but...

Have another little sherry, dear, you might as well.

Nice settled, mature people is what I go for nowadays. Commercials, business people. And I like the male PGs to have a little grey at the temples. I always think a little grey at the temples looks ever so distinguished, don't you? Or bald. They're comfortable, are balds. And jolly...but in a refined way, if you follow me.

Now, with ladies, it's harder. You never really know where you are with lady PGs. I'm saying that against my own sex. I know that. But I might as well be truthful. The truth never hurt anyone. Speak as you find, that's my motto. And it's what I've found, dear, over the years. To be completely frank and honest, I'd as soon have men only in the house. Is that a terrible thing for a woman living on her own to say? Are you shocked? Well, I'm just going on experience. There's no substitute for experience, is what I always say.

They've come here, some of them, very flash, the height of respectability...or so I thought. But I was proved wrong, my dear.

And foreigners. I don't hold with foreigners. Don't get me wrong, I'm not prejudiced or anything like that, mind. But I have my reasons. No...give me your good old English any day. Not too old, of course. But with a little grey at the temples. Or your bald.

There...another little drop will do us no harm. It's only a thimbleful. Cheers, my dear.

I went in for foreigners once. Foreigners and Irish. You can't call the Irish foreigners really, now can you? They're not foreign foreign, if you get my meaning. But trouble! Half the time cleaning out the rooms was spent getting rid of the empties. Used to be embarrassed in front of the dustmen of a Tuesday. And...a bit sad, I found them. Funny that! They're supposed to be a jolly lot. Well, it just wasn't my experience. Oh, yes, when the drinks were flowing, they were jolly enough. A bit too jolly. And generous - I'll give them that. Always invited you to a glass, if you happened to be passing the door. Or if you called for the rent. Either noisy, drunk or sad, that's how I found the Irish. No in-between.

And as for what you might call real foreigners...I had two Italians once. Oh, very respectable. He was a doctor.

First floor return. Middle-aged. Dr. Ostia. She was a widow woman, like myself. Dressed younger, though. A bit...flamboyant. Good figure, if going a little to flesh. But they do, dear, don't they? It's the food, I expect. Macaroni and that. Well, Mrs. Riccini - that was her name, the widow - she had the room second floor front, number 5. Been there about three months. Could be a bit excitable sometimes. Over nothing. But you know how they are. They're like that, aren't they? Although, mind you, the doctor wasn't. Very cool, he was.

Well, wait till I tell you, my dear: one day I was coming down the stairs when I heard this moaning coming from Mrs. Riccini's room. A kind of low moaning. Oooooooooh. Like that. Oooooooooh. I knocked on the door. "Are you all right in there, Mrs. Riccini?" I asked. No answer. I knocked again. The moaning went on. Oooooooooh. I thought she might be in some sort of trouble, might have taken a turn. So I just opened the door and walked in. Well! There she was, sitting - or, rather, flopped - in the armchair, moaning to herself. Oooooooooh. And not a stitch on her! Well, of course, she was quite within her rights. It was her room, after all. She didn't even look up when I came in. It was then I saw what had happened. A piece of plaster from the ceiling in the corner. Must have hit her on the head when she was dressing and gave her a fright. Meant to have that fixed. Knew it was ready to come. But it was only a small piece. And she was going on. Excitable, you see...they're like that. Must have come right down on her head, poor dear. Took no notice of me whatsoever, good, bad or indifferent. Might as well not have been there. Oooooooooh. Moan, moan. I began to get a little frightened myself, I can tell you. Suppose she had concussion, or something? A lot of responsibility, are PGs.

Of course it came to me in a flash...call Dr. Ostia. His room was just on the return. Did I tell you that, dear? I did. Well. He came out in his dressing gown. "Dr. Ostia," I said, "would you come and see to Mrs. Riccini?" He walked into Mrs. Riccini's room, very cool, like, and there I was standing like a fool behind him. And her with nothing on. Still, I didn't mind, him being a doctor and all. He soon had her quietened down. Just took one look and then swept the table-cloth off the table and left it over her in the chair. Without a word. Well, being an Eye-tie himself, you see, he knew how to handle her. That, and being a doctor. Well, it stands to reason.

Anyway...I soon thought of Miss Grey upstairs. Poor Miss Grey. She had the room over Mrs. Riccini's and her bed was in the same corner. I didn't fancy the idea of her coming down, bed and all, through the ceiling. So I went up and knocked at her door. After a minute she opened it and stood there looking at me, groggy, like, and I said to myself, she's been taking the pills again. And she hadn't a stitch on either! True. I thought I was in a blooming nudist colony. So I said, "We'll have to shift your bed, Miss Grey. The plaster's coming off the ceiling in the room below. Mrs. Riccini got a bang on the head." It was then I noticed she wasn't alone in the room. Yes! There was a man trying to cover himself up in the bed. The bedclothes were mostly on the floor and he was snatching at them. Middle-aged, he was, with a stupid-looking red face on him.

Well...I could only come to my own conclusions about Miss Grey. Mind you, I'm not a narrow-minded woman myself. Well, I wouldn't be, married three times, as I told you, now would I? But a funny thing happened two days before - that's right, on the Wednesday, I was cleaning outside on the front steps. This man comes over to me and without so much as a "Good morning" or "Excuse me" he says: "Do you know you have a prostitute living in your house? Better watch out. The police are keeping an eye on her. Three pounds she charges." You could have floored me.

I was just getting my breath, what with the shock and the bending down to clean the steps and all. "How dare you speak about one of my tenants like that?" I says, but I was talking to myself, my dear. He just said his little piece - oh, extremely impolite, he was - and walked round the corner.

Well...I hadn't mentioned this to Miss Grey at all. She was a nice poor soul and we got on very well together. She always looked so tired, poor thing. I used to feel sorry for her and bring her a cup of tea in the mornings when I was doing the room. But the next morning - the Saturday, it was, I was collecting the rents - no, I tell a lie, it was the Thursday, I was just doing the cleaning. I told her straight out. We were having a cup of tea together...I always brought up one for myself to keep her company. I told her what the man said, about her being a prostitute and all. She didn't get upset or annoyed or anything like that, only looked at me as calm as you like with those sad eyes she had, poor thing, and she said: "Yes, Mrs. Clarke, I am a prostitute." I said, "Miss Grey," I said, "I don't believe it." "But I am, Mrs. Clarke," said she. "You surely don't come in here with men, Miss Grey," said I. "I do, Mrs. Clarke," said she. "How could you, Miss Grey?" said I. "Well, I do, Mrs. Clarke," said she, "I had three here last night." "You didn't, Miss Grey," said I. "I did, Mrs. Clarke," said she, "I charge three pounds," said she. "I know that, Miss Grey," said I.

And then I told her: "I suppose you know what this means, Miss Grey," said I. "I'll leave at the end of the week, Mrs. Clarke," said she, very quiet and serious. Poor thing. I felt for her. Wasn't a bit of harm in her. Not really.

What a week that was, my dear, what a week! Dr. Ostia and Mrs. Riccini left on the same Saturday...together! Eloped, my dear. At their age! Three rooms I had to fill, all at the same time.

Oh, it's not easy being a landlady, my dear. It's not all a bed of roses, you know.

He must have seen something he liked...before he covered her up with the table-cloth. The doctor, my dear.

Have another little sherry. Go on, that's right, it'll do you good.

The Song of the Long-Legged Queen
(from BOOKS OF BALE)
John Arden

Books of Bale is a story of four hundred years ago, the time when Queen Elizabeth was trying to conquer Ireland.

In this part of the tale, a young English musician called Lucretia (who lives with an English poet called Tony Munday) meets an Irish sailor in a London pub. He is singing a song in Irish; she thinks it is a lovely air, but she cannot understand the words. She asks him if he knows any English words for it. He says he does, and he will sing them for her.

He said: "I should tell you, ma'am, this song was first made by Proinsias Dubh Ó Dálaigh - you might know him as Francey Daly? - a great poet of my people who is after dying these twelve years in the Kerry war. I should tell you he was in Rome the time he put it together, and 'tis said it was a Roman lady he had in his thought. But there are those that say, no: she was in Ireland, the woman he sang of, and he made both words and air as a memory of her, so. Here's how it goes to start with."

O she walked all in sunshine
and she danced in the rain
And her face in the sunshine
was covered with a veil
A veil of fine muslin
and linen and pale silk
She shook it like the grey ash-tree
does be blowing on the hill.

But when the rain fell
and her dancing began
She lifted it off from her face
and was fully to be seen.
And who was there to see it?
there is no one to tell
For the long-legged woman
danced all by herself.

She danced to take me prisoner
to tie my heart to those hearts
Who led me to the fighting,
put the blade into my belt,
And forbade me to pull it
till I came to the wide brown field
Where the long-legged woman
would bring my foe to me.

Oh who did she bring
but herself and all alone?

So sorrowful a long-legged woman
was never to this day seen.
"You must kill me, pretty soldier,"
was all that she could croak.
Like wine of the land of France
the blood ran from her bent white neck.

O Rome of the priests
and Spain of the silver
And Burren-slope of flowers
that scarcely know hard winter,
Not all of your lovely beauties
can ever make up for me
The long-legged woman
whom I espied but never did see.

"I dare say, ma'am, being put into the English - my own words, do you see, for the English sailors? - it'll not be altogether the class of song you'd understand. I mean, the tale and story of it in a manner of speaking is a hidden one, but that was always the way with Ó Dálaigh, so it was... The Burren hill lies over from Galway, I thought I should tell you that. Ó Dálaigh lived there."

Lucretia learned the song very quickly, but never was able to sing it like the young Irishman sang it. Munday's love-making that night was no good: he said the song had upset him.

"My God, Tony, that's no reason why *you* should upset *me*." Lucretia was growing unhappy, cross with him. It was not long before they parted.

Corcomroe
Edmund Lenihan

Stony in its silent valley
far from the troubled crowd
the time-flecked walls of Corcomroe
wear their quietness like a shroud.

Soft lie all the ages here
that have buried the names of kings
since Donal of the burning eye
sought grace at the well that springs

from the rocks above Oughtmáma
in the shadow of Turlough Hill,
found the quiet that gives these Burren stones
their mournful magic still.

Soft in their tree-lined valley,
lost to the rushing crowd,
the forgotten walls of Donal Mór
wear all the ages out.

The Word "Stone"

John F. Deane

John Twin Fadian watched his head mirrored in the clear water of a rock pool. He opened his mouth and saw the word come out like a stone and plop into the water. "Cloouuurck!" was the sound he made. It was like the beginning of a cough, John Twin's tongue being too big for his mouth, the sounds getting stuck somewhere between his chest and the roots of his tongue. Tony, his twin brother, could speak perfectly; but then Tony was ordinary in every way, normal, uncrooked, having come out first, John reluctantly following.

By late morning the ocean would have come in again and covered this pool, disturbing the life established there, adding new life and the nourishment of algae. It was marvellous. John Twin could sound so many of the words in his mind, so many things that were swimming around or floating or just holding on in the miniature ocean of the pool, or in the wider world of the Atlantic. Words like anemone, periwinkle, barnacle, crab, sea slug, dead-men's-fingers, kelp - these words were delicious sea-words that made him salivate between the teeth, filling his mouth with their salt taste, sparkling like sunlight on the ocean of his brain.

He watched the blob of an anemone, its dark plum-coloured shape, minuscule tentacles plucking algae from the water. It was important to be able to put words on things, John Twin knew, to be able to pick out nourishment from the awful mess that is the universe and name it in its accessible parts, divide it into manageable proportions of actual truth, take it into his soul and refer to it, even if only in the echo-chamber deep within himself.

He put his hand into the water, watched it change shape under the surface, become distorted. He laughed out loud at the funny twist of it. "Arm," he sounded the word deep in his mind, "arm, hand, fingers," but they did not really look like his arm and hand and fingers, not there, shimmering, corkscrewed by the water. Sometimes the words did not quite tally with the objects, then that could be funny - or it could be a lie. He reached for a stone he could see on the bottom of the pool; the floor was further than he had thought and the rolled-up sleeve of his shirt became wet as he reached. He grasped the stone and drew it out. It was beautiful, "stone", hard and true, smoothed by waves, fretted until it had become this shape - like a large egg.

John Twin laughed again. Perhaps, he thought, if I sit on it long enough it will hatch out into a whole lot of little stones. He put it into the pocket of his waistcoat, picked up his bucket and began to clamber over the rocks of the shore towards the sea's edge.

Above his head a black-backed gull swooped towards him, letting out a screech of anger or surprise.

"Cloouuuurck!" it screamed at him.

"Clooooouuuurck!" John shouted back at the bird

and he shook his fist into the air. The gull flew away, out over the waves, clean and big and lovely.

How good to be alive on such a sun-filled morning, the world alert all about him, the sun sparkling on rock and wrack, on cliff and field, over rock pool and ocean; each sparkle was different and each sparkle lovely in its own way. He was looking for barnacles and edible periwinkles, perhaps some moss for the making of puddings. Since his father had left for Coventry in search of work over three years ago and had never returned, the Fadian family were poor indeed. He imagined the dinner they could have, purely from the generosity of the sea: a soup from the remains of yesterday's pollock, a meal of barnacles and periwinkles boiled in milk, a dessert of carrageen moss to delight their bodies and enliven their souls. It would form his contribution today to the family income.

John filled the can, listening always to the infinitely slow movement of the barnacle shells against the aluminium walls; a sad sound, a knocking, a pleading... but they were innocent creatures, they knew nothing of death, they knew nothing of the harsh struggle that a poor family has to make to survive in this land, they didn't even know the word "barnacle", they knew nothing; perhaps, John thought for a moment, perhaps they were the lucky ones...

He turned for home. He left the shore and climbed into Harte's field. He followed a roughly-walled path round the edge of the field, naming buttercup and cowslip and daisy, wondering about the name- "cowslip." Does a cow really... or perhaps it was cow's lip, the little flower just reaching high enough to be ripped out by the moist hardness of the cow's lip? He must watch them the next time he saw Harte's cows in the field. Over the ditch, onto the rough road leading up to the main road. It was Sunday; people would be at Mass, muttering words they hardly understood, words they had mouthed so often they were now empty shells, their juices evaporated.

He came as far as the yard of the Church at the edge of the village. The people were inside; there were some who had taken up their stations leaning against the wall on either side of the great, wooden door outside. They would stay there until the last words were said and then they would go home, or to the pub. John Twin liked to join them, to lean against the wall alongside them. They laughed often, softly, they said funny things, they cracked jokes and he could laugh as heartily as any of them. Sometimes, too, they joked at him, but he didn't mind. They knew his angers, knew, too, that he was strong enough to make them know his feelings if he needed to, even if he couldn't say it to them in words. He heard the voice of the Canon inside, "Twenty-first Sunday in ordinary time...In the beginning..."

The murmuring of the men, the warmth of the sunshine, the exertions of the shore, made John drowsy. He leaned back against the wall and dozed. But then he came to with a start, the men around him buzzing with excitement. A black Mercedes had drawn up outside the low periphery wall of the Church yard, and several men had got out. They were well dressed, wore suits and had hats. One of them held a number of printed sheets. Then another was helped up onto the wall while loudspeaking equipment, speakers, a microphone, were being set up. John Twin loved the sound of the static, the "testing, testing, onetwothreefour, onetwothreefour" that was spoken before everything was ready. It was the Fianna Fail politician for this part of the county, Edward J. Finn. There was going to be some sort of election coming soon.

When people came out from Mass they formed little groups in the yard of the Church. Now there was music playing through the loudspeaker; it seemed to build everyone into some sort of expectancy. The music stopped. One of the men stood up beside Finn and began to shout into the microphone.

"Ladies and gentlemen, may I have your attention please! It gives me great pleasure to introduce..."

John Twin Fadian looked into his can; the mass of black and brown shells was still heaving slowly. He should have put some sea-water in along with them; they would be suffering in the sunshine. He could see the feelers searching, the eyes out on sockets, he could sense their wonderment, the dismay of the poor creatures. Soon he would have to get home, soon, but first he would share some of the excitement in the Church grounds.

Finn was standing at the microphone. He raised his right hand into the air in a gesture of triumph, then his left, then he lifted both hands together and shook them tightly over his head as if he had just won some boxing contest. He drew a half-hearted ripple of applause out of the waiting people.

"My dear friends, my fellow Mayomen, my fellow Irishmen! I am deeply honoured to be here amongst you this lovely morning, and to share in your prayers and to stand in the grounds of your lovely Church. It is always a pleasure to be with you on this your lovely island, a place of true beauty, famous throughout Ireland, and indeed famous much farther afield, in every country around the world."

John Twin thought of his father in England; perhaps he was not in England any more, perhaps he had moved on to Cleveland, in America, where a lot of his friends would be. Someone standing near to John muttered, "The oul' cod! He hasn't been on the island since the last election."

"You know, my dear friends, that there is an election coming a month from now and I am here this morning to ask you to support my party in that election. I have been your representative in Dáil Éireann now for several years and you have seen your prosperity grow during those years. You have seen the tourists come in their thousands, nay, I would suggest, in their hundreds of thousands, to enjoy your hospitality. You have seen the wealth of this nation grow along with the wealth of your lovely island."

Somewhere there was a loud guffaw among the listeners. John Twin looked to see who had laughed. His brother Tony stood in a group of men nearby. John grinned over at him. "Clourck!" he whispered.

"I am here to ask you to give your vote, your number one vote to Sean Frayne in the coming election and I can promise you that he will help you, he will help me, he will help us all, towards that great future you see before you."

Once again Finn raised his fist over his head and punched the air in emphasis. There was a little applause, some shuffling. An old man standing near John muttered, not loudly enough to be heard, "and what about the fishermen, why are they being forced to stop their fishing? Why don't you stop the Spanish from trawling the fish out of our seas?" John nodded his head vigorously. He elbowed the man beside him and nodded towards the politician, but the old man only winked at him.

"We are doing everything possible to make this lovely country even more prosperous. You have seen our country take its place among the nations of Europe."

His fist pounded at the sky.

"In this country the family has always been number one. And we in Fianna Fail have a proud record of fighting for the sanctity of the Irish family."

Someone shouted from the back of the crowd: "And what about emigration?" John Twin grunted his approval of the question.

"I say the family, the Irish family, we shall tend its sanctity, its primacy, against the forces that would destroy it. And Sean Frayne will continue this great crusade, together we will stand firm against every attempt to subvert the Irish family. This I stand for, this I insist upon, for this I will go on fighting!"

Finn's voice had risen high. The well-dressed men standing beside him cheered and applauded; John Twin grunted. One of the periwinkles in his can had worked its way up the side and was about to climb over the rim; John twitched it back down again. He was wondering where the prosperity was. Someone else shouted from the crowd: "Why don't you bring our people home?" The shout was answered by a long chorus of approval. John spoke his word, quietly, "Clouuuurck!"

"We are doing everything possible to bring our emigrants home. They are exiles from this fair land and we are going to set up an agency to look into their problems. We are creating employment at home and it will not be long before the people, our people my dear friends, come to know that their place is here, at home, with their families."

John thought of his mother and her misery, of their home, its poverty, its limited and limiting wholesomeness, of their few unploughable, sodden fields, of the dinner he would make for them all. Why should his father come home to that...why wouldn't they give his mother the money she needed...she fought for it, but she got nothing...he was not telling the truth, up there on the wall.

The other men were moving among the people, handing out leaflets. One of them passed near John, reached a leaflet towards him, then smiled and drew it back, offering it instead to the old man at John's side. John snarled and grabbed the leaflet. He gazed at what he had in his hand: a picture of E. J. Finn, smiling, well-fed, smug, and underneath it a photograph of Sean Frayne and a vote-number-one demand. John looked up at the man on the wall. In his brain something had begun to seethe. It was like the tide coming to stir up the crevices in the rocks; there was a sense of anger, he wanted to name that anger. He tried to shout but all that came from his mouth was a low growl; the frustrations of his life seemed to burst on him like spray from a wave. He trembled, he tried again to shout his anger but the man was loud now, confusing, he was surrounded by a haze of scarlet light, his body seemed to have grown enormous on the wall, to be swollen like a thundercloud, to be darkening the sky. John could not even get his inarticulate sound to come out.

Then the can fell from his grasp and the living mollusks spilled out between the feet of the people. Several were squashed at once and John dropped to his knees to save what he could of his work. The tears were blinding him, people jostled him, walking on the shells that exploded with little crackling sounds. The stone he had picked up from the rock pool fell onto the ground before him.

John Twin Fadian grew still and calm. He picked up the stone and stood erect. He could feel the smoothness and the weight of the stone, he thought of it again as an egg containing within it a myriad of tiny stones. It would burst, it would hatch beautifully against the head of the liar. He heard the sound deep within his brain, "stone", strong, immediate, truth. He drew back his arm and flung it with all his strength and saw it fly straight and true towards its mark.

The Hymn of the Magpie
Michael D. Higgins

The magpie is a peasant bird,
Vulgar,
Hard,
With gaudy bright
Colours,
Beautiful.

A life of stealing
Is revealed
In baubles,
All gathered for their shining
Loveliness.

We are magpies,
Condemned to be despised,
Gatherers of lovely bits
Of knowledge,
No purity left,
No elegant
Isolated nest
Reared us.

We are the birds of the loud screech,
One for bad luck,
Two for good luck.
They count us
The vulgar
Of the streets,
Noisy with our gaudy knowledge
And we can never be
An elegant bird,
Classy,
With a single refined note.

But, there are times
When the light shines
On our bright feathers.
In those moments,
We are beautiful.

A Man I Must Meet

(Excerpt from the Radio Series: Parnell)
G.P. Gallivan.

THE IRISH LEADER, PARNELL, *has been upsetting most of England, particularly the Members of Parliament, by keeping Parliament to long hours because of his campaign to obstruct and block the passing of legislation. One of these MPs, Baxter, and his wife Lydia are walking in the park.*

LYDIA : What a glorious day...the park is so beautiful.

BAXTER : Yes, I should avail of it more often.

LYDIA : You could do with colour in your cheeks.

BAXTER : You can blame Parnell for that. He has us tied to the House.

LYDIA : That man....a born trouble maker!

BAXTER : But a damned smart one.

LYDIA : I find it outrageous that he can bring Parliament to its knees.

BAXTER :Not alone Parliament my dear...the whole

country.

LYDIA : (Indignantly.) Because no one will stand up to him.

BAXTER : It's difficult. He knows his way around all the rules and procedures of the House.

LYDIA : That's no excuse!

BAXTER : (Mildly.) Yes my dear.

LYDIA : (Angrily.) Now none of that; I will not be patronised. Anyway, what kind of man is he...as a person ?

BAXTER : A strange chap....cold, reserved, clinical. Not at all what one expects an Irishman to be.

LYDIA : (Disdainfully.) Oh nothing surprises me where they are concerned. (Breaks off.) Oh Robert look! See who's coming this way.

BAXTER : Who ?...Ah yes, O'Shea and his wife.

LYDIA : I was at school with her...Now isn't that interesting?

BAXTER : (Sarcastically.) That she's an old school friend?

LYDIA : (Impatiently.) You know what I mean. They may be husband and wife but it's common knowledge that they maintain separate establishments.

BAXTER : He has political ambitions. It seems that, for appearances sake, she has agreed to host his dinner parties.

LYDIA : A little odd, don't you think?

BAXTER : Well, she is a charming woman.

LYDIA : (Bitchily.) Men !

BAXTER : Though I'm given to understand that her main attraction for O'Shea these days lies in her inheritance.

LYDIA : Really ?

BAXTER : There's some old aunt in the background. Once she snuffs it the lady is in clover.

LYDIA : Ssh..they'll hear you. (Raising her voice.) We must do this more often Robert. It's such a shame not to when....Why Katie...Willie...what a delightful surprise.

KATIE : Lydia Baxter! And...Robert...is it not ?

BAXTER : You have a good memory, Mrs O'Shea.

O'SHEA : A stroke of luck running into you like this.

KATIE : Willie is right, I am seldom in town these days. It's usually to entertain a few of his associates or to visit the theatre.

LYDIA : Then you mustn't miss the Lyceum. Irving is in splendid form.

KATIE : But I'm told that the best entertainment on view is in the House of Commons with Mr. Parnell in the leading role.

LYDIA : Don't speak to me about that man !

BAXTER : Gently my dear, Willie is a member of the faithful.

O'SHEA : (Quietly.) Just a member of his Party.

LYDIA : Well, I don't mean to offend you...but I think the fellow is a boor.

KATIE : Then you have already met him ?

BAXTER : (Sarcastically.) Certainly not. Lydia never puts her prejudices at risk.

KATIE : (Amused.) Never? As a general rule perhaps...but there must be exceptions. Take Parnell...

LYDIA : (Distainfully.) Oh no.

KATIE : I must confess that I find him intriguing. In fact, I'd quite like to meet him.

LYDIA : Katie ! You can't be serious ?

KATIE : Why not ? I have every intention of meeting him. To judge for myself.

BAXTER : That mightn't be as easy as you think. He is not one for socialising.

O'SHEA : (Amused.) Katie will find a way, she can be most persuasive. We are inviting him to dinner.

KATIE : Perhaps you might care to join us ?

LYDIA : Heaven forbid. You really must reason with her, Willie.

O'SHEA : Quite useless I assure you. Once Katie gets the bit between her teeth...

KATIE : That's it. I can never resist a challenge.

BAXTER : And that's what he'll be. A man who can discipline the Irish Party and turn the whole country on it's ear has got to be ruthless and demanding.

LYDIA : There! Not at all the kind of man you'd wish to know.

KATIE : (Laughing.) Quite the contrary Lydia, the more I hear, the more curious I become. I simply have to meet him.

Cliché
Celia de Fréine

I want to walk along
a wide expanse of beach
with you,
feel the spray
in my face,
no - that's a wild notion,
I'd settle for Killiney's stones
or the winding path
along Howth Head
just the two of us,
walking,
talking,
getting through,
because you are
one of the few
on my wavelength.
Yet you have chosen
to walk away,
not realising
that magic
such as ours
is not easily found -
for most it comes
once in a lifetime, if at all.

A Day in Sicily
Hugh Weir

"I'm sure that's a member of the Mafia," said Maire, pointing to a large man with a cigar in his mouth, and a drooping moustache. He wore white shorts and a very white shirt, as he leant with his behind on the bonnet of his posh white Fiat car. "But members of the Mafia wouldn't be driving Fiats," retorted Joe.

"I bet you," replied Maire who was sure that she knew all about Italians.

Joe and Maire were on their way over the Straits of Messina to Sicily. They had never been there before, but they had read about it in the papers. Joe had said that he'd like to go somewhere new for his holiday, and Maire felt that it could not be too bad as it was near Rome. They had booked with the travel agent down the road. After doing so, they had felt that they should find out more. They got all the booklets and posters they could find and wrote to the Italian Embassy. They went to Italian films. And they learned about the Mafia. The Mafia were dangerous. The

Mafia murdered people. The Mafia had every person in Italy under control. They read that they should keep clear of the Mafia, even if they were Irish.

But here on the ferry across the Straits of Messina was obviously one of the Mafia. Maire held on to her handbag. Even Joe was now feeling a little uncomfortable for he checked his wallet in his pocket and placed both his hands firmly in his main trouser pockets.

As they approached the Sicilian mainland, they leaned over the ship's rails to view the port and watch other ferries on their way back. Where they stood was a kind of metal platform about one metre wide. And there in the middle was the white Fiat and the pensive "Mafia" man.

The ferry berthed and everybody made their way onto land. There were crowds of people including Joe and Maire. Most made their way up the hill to the centre of Messina city. The two followed the rest. Children, youths and others bumped into them for they were slower. The main streets were full of traffic too, and it didn't stop for anybody. They were nervous. After a lot of stops they came to some shops. As they looked in the window of one, Maire screamed, "Help, I've been robbed!"

Maire's handbag had been opened and was empty. Her passport was gone. Her keys were gone. Her cards had been taken, and her money.

"I didn't trust that man," she said. "He was watching everyone. He must have had people working for him. They're all Mafia!"

Joe was stunned. He could say nothing. In the end he softly suggested that they should go to the police station and report the loss.

It was not hard to find the police. The word in Italian is like the one in English. It was quite like a Garda station with stone floors and dark wooden desks. It was cool and the echoes of boots and loud talk rang as men marched about.

"Por favore," Maire said to the dark blue uniformed man behind the counter, "I've been robbed."

Joe said little.

Maire told the policeman about her problem. But she did not tell him about the Mafia. Two others joined in the talk, loudly arguing with each other. In the end, she was asked to go with all three. Joe was ordered to stay. He sat down on a hard bench to one side of the main hall.

The four, Maire and the three policemen, made their way down a long cool tiled passage. At the end was a larger door than the rest. It had a notice with times on it. One of the men knocked. There was no sound. He knocked again.

"Come in," shouted a voice in Italian.

The door opened into a huge well furnished room with a large desk in the middle. Behind it was a chair. Maire blushed. Who should be sitting on the chair but the man of the white Fiat, cigar and all.

"I've only just got in. What can I do for you?" he said.

One of the policemen let out a stream of Italian words.

The "Mafia man" took down notes and then turned to Maire. "This is not an easy world; you must suspect everybody as being a prospective criminal. We'll do our best, but in future, please hold onto your bag."

Maire hadn't the courage to tell him that she had even suspected him. When she got back to Joe, she was happy to tell him that she had been right to suspect everyone. The rest of their visit was happier as several policemen waved at them, not knowing that their own boss had been suspect.

Sunset
Mark Hutcheson

Juice sparkled round your chin
from those grapes you guzzled on the fountain
in a square darkening, deserted by its heat.
Shoeless urchins still skirmished in doorways
against the ivy, kicking a football.

There you sat with your legs dangling
contented like the child you were perhaps
some twenty rubbed-out years ago
and slowly smiled at me.
Few sunsets are as beautiful.

For Petra Kelly

Frank McGuinness

I think the sun is crying,
The earth shines in its eyes.

I hear the sea being quiet.
The continent's on fire.

I think the sea is crying,
The earth and sun and fire.

The Crime
Albert Crawford

I was helping my father to put up a greenhouse at the top of his garden. My six year-old son, Keith, was burning dead potato stalks, a little way down. I watched the sheer joy on his face as the flames rose and the smoke swirled around him. That swirl of smoke took me back thirty years to Castlecaulfield, with Mickey and the gang.

Our favourite sport was lighting whins. That September evening, we were up in the high fields of Patterson's farm. From bush to bush we sped. Mickey with the matches, lighting, shouting, running from one to the next. As each blaze burst forth we whooped and danced like wild Indians around their war fires.

Whin burns easily and brightly, but it does not last long and soon we were high on the hillside, right in view of the farmhouse.

"Away out of that, ye bundle of wee skitters!" roared the voice, and Mr. Patterson rushed through a gap, waving an ash plant over his head. In those days, children did not talk back to their elders, for those elders knew how to use their sticks. We ran for our lives.

But, half an hour later, with the autumn light pale upon the hillside, five small figures crept back up along the smouldering bank of blackened whins. The Castlecaulfield Indians had returned, and this time it was the haystacks we had in mind.

We screwed hay into torches, and in seconds the first stack was alight. We darted to the next, and by the time the third was blazing we were drunk with the roar of those flames. Whooping and yelling, the Indian braves danced once more around the war fires. The hay burned much longer than the whins. Our eyes smarted with the smoke. We chased flying embers. Sparks singed our hair. We were burning the white man's cabins, and loving it.

The roar of the man and gun came together. Shot spattered the trees behind us. In the same instant, we were off like arrows from a bow. We leaped the remains of Patterson's smouldering hedge, raced low along the sheugh, climbed the gate and landed in the ploughed field.

But how does a four year-old run over a ploughed field? My young brother, Mervyn, tried but he stumbled and nearly fell. Lead shot tore the ground behind us. The farmer bellowed like one of his own bulls. Another shot rang out.

"Up on my back, Mervyn!" cried Mickey. "Come on. Quick! Up with you."

My brother leaped, clung round his neck, and we were off again, across the ruts of hard soil, and through the hedge into the lane. We bounded down it, climbed the style into the moss and down to the main road and away.

My father was the police sergeant in those days and, of course, he investigated that crime.

"Ill-reared young pups," he said to my mother the next day. "I'll find out who they are, and when I catch them, they'll not sit down for a while. Imagine destroying a man's hay."

Mervyn and I sat like little angels and ate up all our rabbit stew. We even asked to be allowed to leave the table. This surprised my mother no end, and when we took our cod liver oil and malt without a word, she wondered if we were ill.

It hardly seemed like thirty years ago. I was smiling to myself as the smoke swirled again, and I saw my son Keith's face, blackened with sooty war paint and glowing with joy as he watched the flames. I turned to my father.

"Do you remember the night Patterson's haystacks were burned?" I asked.

"Indeed I do," he said. "I remember it well."

I was still smiling. "You never solved that crime?" I said, looking straight at him.

He took a pull on the pipe, scratched his chin with the stem and looked down at Keith's black, smiling face.

"That's the boy," he said to him. "Rake in all those wee bits. They make a great fire."

Then he pointed the pipe at me.

"No," he said thoughtfully, "you're quite right. I never solved that crime, and don't you forget it."

Scarecrow

(For John)
Sara Berkeley

I danced with a man of straw
The music blew through his prickly arms
His heart was a reed
It went with the wind,
His smile was wry, tinderish to the touch
There were seeds for teeth
I could hear the pods cracking
As he lit a song.
We danced for a week, I was danced dry
I heard the changes being rung in me
And had I been a bird
I, too, would have risen with a shrill, vowel sound.

The Followers

Maura Treacy

"For Heaven's sake," Celia said, "don't they ever talk about anything else?"

It was four hours since the match had ended. Celia had just made her way through a roomful of men who didn't even notice when she brushed against them. She set three full glasses down on the table.

"Where did you leave the lads?" Pheenie asked. Her laugh was getting sharper all the time.

"They left me," Celia said. She put down the vodka she was about to drink. On second thoughts, she would not drown her resentment.

Alice was leaning forward, her eyes shining, eager to be part of the celebration. As she picked up the fresh glass of orange, she realised that neither her sister nor Pheenie shared her enthusiasm. Quietly she sat back in line with them.

As far as Alice could see, the only surprise was that Richie hadn't broken away from Celia much earlier in the day.

After the match, when everyone else was crowding onto the field to get near the players and to carry them on their shoulders, Celia had taken Richie firmly by the elbow. She led him away from all the grinning, flag-waving people they knew who were waiting to see their team presented with the Cup; instead, they joined the losers and others who had begun to leave before the match ended, when the result was already clear.

"Jay, we might as well have lost!" Richie protested when he saw himself being led away from the moment of victory.

"We've had enough of it," Celia said. "What else is there to see? Come on!"

They heard someone calling them.

"Celia! Richie!"

They looked up. Pheenie Walsh was standing five rows above them. She rushed down the steps to them.

"Oh, hello, Alice!" she said. "I didn't see you - sent along to keep an eye on your big sister, were you?"

"When did you get back?" Celia asked.

"Oh, yesterday evening! Wouldn't you know! We were just in time to meet the team as their train came in!"

"Oh, the hard man - Tom!" Richie laughed. He ignored Celia. "It was the last thing he said that morning before the wedding: 'Don't worry,' he said, 'whatever else I'll be back, Spain or no Spain, I'll be home for the Final. Depend on that.' "

"If we were half as dependable for getting to the church on time," Pheenie said.

"He was there before yourself, all the same," Richie pointed out. "Isn't that all that's wanted?"

"True," Pheenie agreed, "but only because I knew

what to expect, so I made sure I wasn't the one who was left waiting. Anyway, tell us, did anything wild happen at home since? How's everyone?"

"Oh, all right," Celia said, "but where is Tom now?"

She looked around for Pheenie's new husband.

"He's gone in on the pitch," Pheenie said, looking around too, but laughing. She could see Tom's head three inches above everyone else's. "He's easy to keep track of, anyway. He wants to be the first to get the captain up on his shoulders."

Richie looked back sadly.

"You're not going away already, are you?" Pheenie teased him. "Sure they're all gone in there now, all the lads. The fun is only starting."

"For whom?" Celia asked.

"Ah, it's a bit of sport, girl," Pheenie laughed.

"Yes," Celia said, "and a bit of sport goes a long way."

She steered Richie away with her. Alice stayed with Pheenie to wait for Tom, and she was glad to be free of Celia and her air of disapproval for the rest of the day.

On the way home, later that evening, it was Pheenie who spotted Richie's car outside the hotel.

"Trust Celia," she said, "to get away from the mob. Come on in and we'll surprise them. Will you look behind!" she said. "They all think we've found a shebeen." One by one several other cars had dropped out of the homebound traffic and followed them into the car park.

They found Celia and Richie in a quiet corner of the lounge. The news in Irish was on television and Richie was leaning forward, hoping for some mention of the match. Celia was relaxed now. She rearranged her bracelet and watch; she smoothed her sweater down over her jeans and admired her figure.

Her satisfied expression changed when the glass door swung open and she heard familiar voices and familiar names.

The door closed again. The next time it swung open there was a man hanging on to it. He was followed by several others and they crowded in around her. Richie tried hard to look as if this was the last thing he'd have wished for. An elderly man sat down beside her, wrapped his arm around her shoulders and asked her what she thought of that for one powerful match?

When the news ended, someone switched off the television. The regular customers were out-numbered; but when drinks were put into their hands, they either joined in the party or left quietly. Richie reached out for a pint and there, as far as Celia was concerned, the day's outing ended.

After that, she moved around the room; she joined one group or another but everyone kept on moving around. Even as she spoke to somebody she knew, he'd interrupt her. "Oh, there's a man I didn't see since morning," he'd say. "Hold on there a minute. I'll be back. I must go and hear what he has to say about it all."

And Alice was in the thick of it, lapping it all up, with that stupid smile on her face. Pheenie was glad just to be back amongst the people she knew. Tom was being treated like a hero.

"You know," they said, "some fellows'd have gone straight home from the airport, and they'd be there now, showing the photos of the honeymoon to the mother-in-law, or gathering up the bits of string off the wedding presents."

"And what's wrong with that?" Celia asked.

Left alone in the midst of the crowd, she wondered who she could join up with.

"Cel-yah?" The voice crept up on her.

"An-drew?" she echoed. Wherever she went, sooner or later Andrew showed up there too.

"Hhh-hh," he tittered - he couldn't be blamed for seizing an opportunity, now could he? Holding the knot of his tie, he wriggled and stretched his neck out of his collar as if to show her that, given a chance, he could be tall enough for her. "Can I get you a drink? Brandy? Anything you like?"

"Drown yourself in it," she hissed and dived into the crowd. She grabbed Alice and told her to stay beside her from there on. Soon they were joined by Pheenie and together they drifted around, too many now to fit into any group.

After a while they found seats in a corner, and there they sat with their drinks, while the men moved around the room, going from one group to another, talking, drinking, back-slapping, sometimes breaking into song or laughter.

"Do you mind if I sit here, girls?"

"No, Kathleen. Hello."

Kathleen sat down beside them, her hands clasped around one knee as she watched the roomful of men.

"Another refugee," Pheenie said. "Who are you with?"

"I'm on my own. I got a lift with some people," she said without taking her eyes off the men. But not one of them seemed to notice her; she was puzzled. She glanced at the other three girls and wondered what they were waiting for.

"You can always take them back and exchange them," Celia was advising Pheenie who had got five weighing scales for wedding presents.

"I'd hate to do that," Pheenie said.

"Well, then you should have made a list and let people know what you wanted," Celia pointed out.

"Ah, sure, what harm." Pheenie was sorry now that she had brought up the subject. She wished she could sit there by herself just watching what was going on, so that she didn't feel the time passing. But sitting beside Celia, she had to say something. One silent woman might look mysterious; two or more tight-lipped women in a corner looked as if they were planning something spiteful.

"Do you colour your hair?" Kathleen asked her suddenly.

"I...do not," Pheenie said.

"I just thought, it's staying very dark."

"I haven't it all that long," Pheenie said reasonably.

"You mean it's a wig! Gor, you'd never know. It's terrific! Honestly!"

"No, dear. It's not a wig," said Pheenie. "That little rip," she said to Celia when Kathleen's attention wandered again. "She'd have you on the pension, the first tooth you lost."

Celia, who had all of hers, gave her widest smile.

Kathleen was getting restless; not one of the men still showed any interest. This time she picked on Alice.

"Where did you buy your sweater? I saw ones the very same, piles of them, in Dunne's last week. But they must have been only in children's sizes or something. Honestly," she complained to them all, "I could hardly get one to fit me across here." She flicked her polished finger-nail back and forth across her chest. "And you hate to be too prominent," she confided.

"Sure you must be mortified," Pheenie said.

The last drinks were being served. Kathleen, tired of waiting, moved out amongst the men.

Tom toppled forward through the crowd and steadied himself against the table.

"Well, ladies," he asked, "what are ye having?"

"The time of our lives," Celia said.

"Isn't it a great bloody night!" He rubbed his hands together. "Are ye enjoying it?"

"Immensely."

"That's good, that's good," he approved. "Ah, there's nothing like it. It's the only night of the year."

"Indeed," Pheenie said; she was beginning to sound almost like Celia.

"And yourself," Tom said to Alice, "you're enjoying it as much as any of them."

"It's her first night out," Celia said, "she'd enjoy anything."

"And are you not having anything better than that?" he asked, picking up her glass of orange, as if some mistake had been made. He turned to look at the shelves of the bar.

"Would you try a gin and tonic? That's a nice drink now - all the women take it. Or a glass of sherry?" he suggested, knowing she'd have seen her mother drink it at weddings and christenings. "Aye, a sherry. Now that wouldn't harm a baby."

"Babies don't run the same risks," Celia said as Alice was about to accept. "She'll have orange again."

"And so will I," Pheenie said. She was sitting back, her arms wrapped around herself, her bare feet spread on the floor; she looked at Tom, calmly, without any illusion. "And we're going home then. Now go and get the drinks. How many times," she said when he was gone, "have I sat in a corner watching that fellow going the rounds, getting more sloshed with everyone he meets, and more talkative with every drink; and then I have to sit into a car with him driving home, taking both sides of the road. Well, I won't complain this time. We're married now. After ten years. I've done my stint, trailing around after him to every dog-fight in the country. Well, this time next year, if God is good and Tom is willing, I'll have a good excuse, or maybe two - did you know that twins run in his family? - to stay at home and watch it in comfort on television. I can sit down with a pot of tea and an apple tart. I'll put my feet up on another chair and I can read the Sunday papers during the dull bits. And Micheál O'Hehir will be there, nice and helpful, to tell me who's scoring and exactly what he's scoring, so I need never again make an ass of myself above in the Hogan stand, trying to get into the spirit of the thing, jumping a foot off the ground and roaring, "A goal! It's a goal!" only to be hauled down and told not to disgrace all belonging to me, that it's a point and Tipperary scored it. And when the match is over I can go for a walk or read a book, and when I'm tired I can go to bed, instead of sitting here getting smoke in my eyes and ruining my kidneys with orange squash."

They were the last to leave the hotel. Richie was standing alone on the steps, watching couples packing into cars and driving away, hooting horns and cheering each other on through rolled-down windows. His coloured paper cap had slipped to one side of his head; on the lapel of his jacket, the tiny doll he'd bought that morning was now in disarray, her paper skirts covering only her face.

Celia passed by him without a word on her way to Tom's car. Pheenie paused to pat his cheek, to arrange the doll's skirts more decently, and to tell him that he couldn't win them all.

Fishing

Daniel P. Stokes

He dangled with care
The swaggering bait:
His crown of blond hair,
Cold confident air,
And words smooth as slate.

Though tempted, near beguiled,
She was hooked once before,
Where she thrashed for a while
In the death of a smile,
At last leapt overboard.

As she just swam 'round
And sniffed at the lure,
The line was rewound.
In his mouth he found
The hook bit secure.

Outpatients
Leland Bardwell

"This way, please. No. Not you dear." The orderly beckoned to Nina. "You," she said. Her voice dropped, not sure whether Nina was next in the queue. Nina held the left elbow in her right fist taking care not to jolt it.

"Have you given your name, dear?"

"No. Not yet."

"Oh," the orderly said. "Then you'd better sit down again."

Nina sat down on the wooden seat. She could see the nuns bustling around beyond the glass partition; they moved separately from each other, some with papers in their hands, all their faces polished. Behind the partition there was no sound; mute sisters of charity.

Hack away the sleeve as the arm swells! But they're in a hurry and won't notice.

Jesus! The bastard's broken it this time! What can she tell them, these remote women? That she is a lousy wife and gets beaten up every so often? So she can't admit it? Must she lie, make up a new story each time, each one more improbable than the last, in order to maintain the core of the myth that marriage works? So that as society believes, the woman is, finally, to blame?

Is that it?

Nina was cold, undernourished, too lightly clad; she was trying not to shiver or laugh or annoy the woman beside her; she looked occasionally into the area beyond the glass partition and wondered would the nuns suddenly gather their papers into their arms and stride towards them - the sick, the destitute.

But she did laugh and the woman, or rather girl, beside her crouched low and shook her head; the pale hair rose and fell like lint on her cheeks.

"They take their time," she said.

Nina read: NO LOITERING. Like the NO SMOK-ING notice it had been, always would be, ignored. They hung around and smoked, their hands curled round the cigarettes, wisps of smoke trailing through the fingers. When the nuns came they would stamp on the cigarettes and put the stubs in their pockets.

She knew it was lucky it was her left arm that he had hit for half an hour. Or it had seemed like that. It had been dole day and he had been drinking all afternoon. He was in the sodden destructive mood that came on him every Tuesday and when he saw Frank, who had just called in, he began.

He'd simply said, "Go!" and Frank had gone and Brendan had picked up the axe handle. Useless her trying to escape, shielding her face with her forearm which took the punishment. She had run round the room, ducked under the table, shouting, "Stop, please stop!"

But it *was* lucky it was her left arm, she thought and

thought about the sewing she needed to do; the middle child, poor kid, no button on his coat and off to school in rubber boots.

How did other mothers keep their children neat, spotless? Why couldn't she? That time Frank came and sat beside them on the canal bank she had been ashamed of their pale grubby faces, the middle one, again holding his coat shut with one hand and fishing for minnows with the other. But a short moment of happiness had come on her when he had put his notebooks on the grass and touched her shoulder.

"You don't say very much," he had said. "But you make me feel intelligent."

"What a strange thing to say," had she said? Or perhaps, "But you are, aren't you?" At any rate they had looked into the canal which was clear and still as a photograph till he'd let go her shoulder to stir the water with a stick and splinter their reflections and she thought he must have been embarassed when he touched her but the touch of his hand on her arm had changed the day, the whole week, even.

The nun had come and was leading the girl beside her down the corridor. It would be her turn soon and she must have her story ready.

Last month it had been a rigmarole about slipping in the wet yard and...

She looked up at the nun who had returned.

"Name?"

A biro was poised over the writing pad.

"Nina Sheridan."

The few details checked, the nun looked at her arm. A precise glance, "How did you get this?"

And now the story must run its course. Nina

remembered some half-prepared sentences:

"I was diving off a jetty at Seapoint and my arm hit off a rock."

"Have you children?"

"Four."

"And where were your children when you were diving into the sea?"

"Playing in the sand."

"Alone?"

"Yes. They were quite safe. You see..."

Nina stood now before the nun; anger had begun to run down her chest. "Yes," she shouted.

"Sit down," the nun said.

It was all wasted, the anger, the accelerated heart-beat; the nun had walked away and Nina had to sit again, alone this time except for a copy of *The Word* which lay half open on the seat beside her.

She would check her fury by reading *The Word*, a magazine which told you facts about people worse off than yourself as opposed to women's magazines which left your mind open to fantasy. She slid her hand over the cover, uneasy, for as yet she was not prepared to admit to the lack of fight that had reduced her own life in essence to the status of some of the women from whom circumstances had removed the last grain of hope. But she was saved from opening it by the return of the nun. She bore upon her with that assertiveness that seemed even worse then than the anger that had now quite left, or worse, even, than the continuous throbbing of her arm.

"First visit?"

"I was here three months ago with a broken nose."

The nun looked away.

"I'm accident prone." Now she could begin to laugh, to ignore.

"I forgot to ask you your address." Nina's arm was picked up and dropped like a stone being quickly replaced on a nest of slugs. The shock of pain lodged under her armpit; tears burnt.

"I'll have to find your file."

Nina worried about the babies; would Brendan mind them or would he just go out and leave them alone?

"Get up, get up for God's sake, you've broken my arm!" Had she said that with authority? Or, "I have to go to the hospital. Mind the children!" Please? Hardly!

There were others lined up now, not least an oldish man with all the emblems of the wino - mac stained from nights on the streets, a man who could never be astonished again, an old rag of a bandage on his hand - here for a dressing, a bit of warmth, a secure telling off.

Nina was invaded by coldness. She wished she could afford paper nappies. For how could she wring out pissy blankets with one broken arm?

"You may follow me." The nun came and went and Nina followed as she strode ahead as though in grand opera. In a small room two patients were already seated. Their expressions laid back, they held charts in their hands. One woman had a plaster cast down her leg which left her five toes bared, inquisitive, impervious to the cold. She wondered how long a fracture would take to heal in her own case? A month? Six weeks? The comedy might continue indefinitely, for how could she take in typing now? Yes, until the fracture knitted they would have to beg Brendan for some of his dole or steal - and not for the first time. She laughed, addressing the woman with the broken leg.

"Have you been here long?"

"I don't know what you're at."

"Are you an In-patient?"

The woman got up painfully, she had been called to the next stage, the pre-X-ray room, to queue again, presumably. The orderly in charge of her turned to Nina.

"You for X-ray?"

"I think so."

"Have you got your card?"

"No."

He herded out the woman on crutches; through the other door. The first nun entered.

"Where's your chart?"

"I haven't got one."

The nun clicked her heels like a soldier on parade. "They keep doing that."

Nina sat on with the second woman who had obscured herself behind a sheet of patience and the nun disappeared once more.

She would give up smoking, save up, buy shoes - those nice Clark's sandals - for the middle child. And walk out to meet Frank on the canal bank, lie in the sun, stir the water, talk of Brendan's cruelty; she became lost in the fraud of fantasy.

"Here's a card!"

The Word tucked under her bad arm, Nina took the card.

"I can't find your chart."

They couldn't take the card away now, she thought. She spoke to the other woman.

"At least I have an identification. Perhaps things will speed up."

"I doubt it," the woman spoke undramatically. "They can change their minds if they like."

"But they have to X-ray me now."

"Don't be too sure about that."

Two nuns entered at last to bring them to the final room.

There, those in the row of patients were mostly in regulation dressing gowns. Their faces were sliced from their bodies by a sly ray of sunshine. Relentless sunshine, showing up the illnesses on each face, making everyone look worse, even, than they were. She counted them - 12. The radiologist must have gone for her elevenses.

Would Brendan feed the baby, she wondered, looking the length of a TWA poster; the girl, chocolate-faced, sipped a blue drink under the shade of a striped umbrella; she was being watched by a young man, his chunky face animated by lust, his skin a lighter shade than the girl's - the colour of cardboard.

But now they were moving; the queue was diminishing; the radiologist must be back from the coffee break. Had she eaten ginger biscuits?

The patients straightened their features each time a nun passed but Nina, not knowing why, could not do so; her lies, her self-protection, created an area of secrecy beyond which others could not travel. This she created in herself aware of its lack of value, good sense.

She thought only of the button missing from the child's coat, even forgetting Frank or her husband, Brendan, the man with whom she sometimes felt she had traded her sanity.

The card fell out of her hand, lay at her feet; a discarded bingo card - squares and numbers - Nina Sheridan, upside down and married. Respectable...

"Mrs. Sheridan!" How had the room emptied suddenly? The few magazines sliding from the rep-covered bench; the woman at her typewriter relaxing; a little coffee spilled on the saucer of an empty cup.

"You may go in now."

She bent for the card to tuck into *The Word*. Careful again not to jolt her arm, aware of the lifting throb as she walked to the door of the X-ray room.

"Did he clout you?"

"Not once but many times." No trace of disapproval on the radiologist's face; as she bent, the clean overall swung open over the fresh cotton of her dress. "Men are beasts!" She smiled, played with her machines. "I'll try not to hurt you. You had a long wait."

Now Nina could state: "Everyone's in the same boat."

"There's no same boat about it. It's the old formula. Take away people's self-reliance. Tell them nothing. Then we give them the soft sell, twenty, thirty times a day."

She brushed Nina's fingers. "Try to straighten them."

A half-moon with the hand was crushed back with the effort.

"Sorry."

"Don't apologise. Just lie there with your arm on the paper. I won't hurt you," she said again.

The shutters of the machine swished.

"That's great. Fine."

So she had shut her eyes, she knew because the face above her swung like a coin in the distance, too far away to touch, for she would have drawn her fingers like a pencil over the contours of the mouth had she been able to reach.

"Perhaps I slept." The radiologist held out a larger than foolscap envelope. "Where do I go now?"

"Home."

"The fracture?"

"Don't worry."

"But the X-rays? May I not see...I mean..."

"I think you are the last this morning. Take your time."

The radiologist was holding the door open watching the tread of the patient's feet into the empty shoes; *The Word* was on the floor again, cover page folded back. A Somali infant stood naked, naval protruding like a rotten grape.

"I dropped my magazine. Or rather it's not mine. It's a good magazine, isn't it?"

Love is so fleeting, Nina thought. So inadequate.

The Nun's Story

Gabriel Fitzmaurice

Home on her first vacation
After sixty-seven years,
She looks around her niece's home;
Her eyes fill up with tears

For there's a photo on the wall
In her niece's bungalow
Of a rebel who was shot nearby
All those years ago.

"Sister, why're you crying?"
Her niece gently enquires.
Her auntie sobs, then blows her nose,
And this is her reply:

"The young man in that photo
And I were to be wed
But he was shot by the Black-and-Tans.
I never shared his bed,

Never bore him children,
Never brushed his floor,
Never called him 'husband'.
I left him on the moor

Surrounded by the enemy;
I couldn't hold his hand
Or kiss him as he lay dying.
I watched from cover as

They threw him in their lorry
And took my love away.
I joined the nuns that summer
And sailed to America.

And there I nursed the dying
For the greater love of God
And there I nursed my manly love
Dying in the bog.

And, when I see that photo,
It brings back all to me,
My only love, my dear, dead love.
Oh, what is liberty?

I live by Christ's example
'Blessed are the poor....'
But he is dead, my Lazarus,
And I can but endure."

The English of Dawson Street

James Liddy

My father had the contract for supplying shoes to all the theatres in Dublin, in Jimmy O'Dea's time. One day Mac Liammoir came to the shop, he wanted white lace boots. Now my father had lace boots alright, but no white pair. Will I ever forget it, Jimmy? I was only about fifteen years of age but I set to work, painting the boots.

At that time Mac Liammoir and Edwards lived on the top of a house in Dawson Street. I remember the stairs, it was peeling and dismal. I made my way up and knocked on the door a long time.

Mac Liammoir opened it, took the boots; he didn't ask me in. Jimmy, he spoke beautiful English, didn't he? You don't hear English like that nowadays, no, not at all.

Advice from Joey the Lips

(from The Commitments)
Roddy Doyle

Jimmy phoned Joey the Lips about a week after The Commitments broke up.

He hadn't tried to get them together again. He hadn't wanted to. They were fuckin' saps. He'd watched telly all week. It wasn't too bad. He'd gone for a few scoops with the lads from work on the Friday. That was his week.

He hadn't gone into The Bailey to meet Dave from Eejit.

He hadn't played any soul.

Now, a week after, he thought he was over it. He'd nearly cried when he was in bed that night. He'd have loved to have seen that Commitments single, with them on the cover, and maybe a video for Anything Goes. But now he was okay. They were tossers. So was Dave from Eejit. He had better things to do with his life.

But he was phoning Joey the Lips, just to say cheerio,

121

and good luck, because Joey the Lips wasn't like the others. Joey the Lips was different. He'd taught them all a thing or two.

Joey the Lips answered.

-The Fagan household.

-Joey? Howyeh. This is Jimmy.

-Jimmy! My main man. How are you, Brother?

-Grand. How's your nose?

-It's still hanging on in there.

-Tha' was a fuckin' terrible thing for Deco to do.

-Forget it, forget it. When I was leaving the hospital they were bringing Brother Declan in.

-Wha'?

-On a stretcher.

-Go 'way! Funny. I haven't seen him since. I'd forgot he works where I work.

-Have you seen the other Brothers and Sisters?

-No way. I don't want to.

-Hmm. A pity.

-Wha' are yeh goin' to do now?

-America calls, Brother. I'm going back. Maybe soul isn't right for Ireland. So I'm not right. I'm going back to the soul.

-When?

-The day after tomorrow. Joe Tex called me. You've heard of Joe Tex?

-I've heard the name alrigh'. Hang on. He had a hit there. Ain't Gonna Bump No More with No Big Fat Woman.

-Correct. Joe wants me to tour with him again.

-Fair play to yeh. Anyway, Joey, I phoned yeh to

thank yeh for everythin', yeh know. So - thanks.

-Oh, I blush. Thank The Lord, not me.

-You thank him for me, okay?

-I will do. Will you continue the good work, Jimmy?

-No way. I've learnt me lesson.

-Hang on one minute.

-Okay.

Joey the Lips was back.

-Howyeh, said Jimmy.

-Listen to this. - *Oh sing unto the Lord, a new song, for he hath done marvellous things. Make a joyful noise unto the Lord, all the earth make a loud noise, and rejoice, and sing praise.* - Psalm Number 98, Brother Jimmy.

-Fuck off, Joey. Good luck.

Jimmy was in the kitchen filling the kettle when he remembered something, something he'd read a while back. Joe Tex died in 1982.

House
Pat Boran

Water clanks from the tap
like a chain - a lifetime

since anything has moved here
but rats and birds. I see

the last inhabitants as a father
and son, the father

sending the son off to the city
with a handshake and a pocket

of old pound notes.
He might as well be sending him

to bring home the time
without a watch to carry it.

The Creamery Manager

John McGahern

The books and files had been taken out. They hadn't
yet stopped him from entering his office. Tired of sitting
alone listening to the rain beat on the iron, he came out on
the platform where he could look down on the long queue of
tractors towing in the steel tanks, the wipers making furious,
relentless arcs across the windscreens as they waited. He
knew all the men sitting behind the glass of the cabs by
name. That he had made his first business when he came to
manage the creamery years before. Often on a wet summer's
day, many of them would pull in below the platform to sit
and talk. The rough, childish faces would look up in a glow
of pleasure at the recognition when he shouted out their
names. Some would flash their lights.

Today no one looked up. He could see them
observing him in their mirrors after they had passed. They
probably already knew more precisely than he what awaited
him. Even with that knowledge he would have preferred if
they looked up. All his life he had the weakness of wanting

to please and give pleasure.

When the angelus bell rang from Cootehall, he began to think that they might have put off coming for him for another day, but soon after the last stroke he heard heavy boots crossing the cement. A low knock came on the door. Guard Casey was in the doorway but there was no sign of the sergeant, Guard Guider was the other guard.

"You know why we're here, Jim," Guard Casey said.

"I know, Ned." Quickly the guard read out the statement of arrest.

"You'll come with us, then?"

"Sure I'll come."

"I'm sorry to have to do this but they're the rules." He brought out a pair of bright handcuffs with a small green ribbon on the linking bar. Guider quickly handcuffed him to Casey and withdrew the key. The bar with the green ribbon kept the wrists apart but the hands and elbows touched. This caused them to walk stiffly and hesitantly and in step. The cement had been hosed clean but the people who worked for him were out of sight. The electric hum of the separators drowned their footsteps as they crossed to the squad car.

In the barracks the sergeant was waiting for him with a peace commissioner, a teacher from the other end of the parish, and they began committal proceedings at once. The sergeant was grim-faced and inscrutable.

"I'm sorry for that Sunday in Clones," the creamery manager blurted out in nervousness. "I only meant it as a day out together."

The grimness of the sergeant's face did not relent; it was as if he had never spoken. He was asked if he had a solicitor. He had none. Did he want to be represented? Did he need to be? he responded. It was not necessary at this stage, he was told. In that case, they could begin. Anything he said, he was warned, could be used against him. He would say nothing. Though it directly concerned him, it seemed to be hardly about him at all, and it did not take long. Tonight he'd spend in the barracks. The cell was already prepared for him. Tomorrow he'd be transferred to Mountjoy to await his trial. The proceedings for the present were at an end. There was a mild air of relief.

Less than a month before, he had bought stand tickets for the Ulster Final and had taken the sergeant and Guard Casey to Clones. He already knew then that the end couldn't be far off. It must have been cowardice and an old need to ingratiate. Now it was the only part of the whole business that made him cringe.

They had set off in the sergeant's small Ford. Guard Casey sat with the sergeant in the front. They were both big men, Casey running to flesh, but the sergeant retained some of an athlete's spareness of feature. He had played three or four times for Cavan and had been on the fringe of the team for a few seasons several years before.

"You were a terrible man to go and buy those stand tickets, Jim," Casey had said for the fifth time as the car travelled over the dusty white roads.

"What's terrible about it? Aren't we all Ulster men even if we are stranded in the west? It's a day out, a day out of all our lives. And the sergeant here even played for Cavan."

"Once or twice. Once or twice. Trial runs. You could hardly call it *played*. I just wasn't good enough."

"You were more than good enough by all accounts. There was a clique."

"You're blaming the selectors now. The selectors had a job to do. They couldn't pick everybody."

"More than me has said they were a clique. They had their favourites. You weren't called the boiler for nothing."

A car parked round a corner forced the sergeant to

swerve out into the road. Nothing was coming.

"You'd think the car was specially parked there to deliver an accident."

"They're all driving around in cars," Casey said, "but the mentality is still of the jennet and cart."

It had been a sort of suffering to keep the talk going, but silence was even worse. There were many small flowers in the grass margins of the roadside.

They took their seats in the stand halfway through the minor game. There was one grace: though he came from close to Clones, there wasn't a single person he knew sitting in any of the nearby seats. The minor game ended. Once the seniors came on the field he started at the sudden power and speed with which the ball was driven about. The game was never close. Cavan drew gradually ahead to win easily. Such was the air of unreality he felt, of three men watching themselves watch a game, that he was glad to buy oranges from a seller moving between the seats, to hand the fruit around, to peel the skin away, to taste the bitter juice. Only once did he start and stir uncomfortably, when Guard Casey remarked about the powerful Cavan fullback, who was roughing up the Tyrone forwards, "the Gunner is taking no prisoners today."

He was not to be so lucky on leaving the game. In the packed streets of the town a voice called out. "Is it not Jimmy McCarron?" And at once the whole street seemed to know him. They stood in his path, put arms around him, drew him to the bars. "An Ulster Final, look at the evening we'll have, and it's only starting."

"Another time, Mick. Another time, Joe. Great to see you but we have to get back." He had pushed desperately on, not introducing his two companions.

"You seem to be the most popular man in town," the sergeant said once they were clear.

"I'm from round here."

"It's better to be popular anyhow than buried away out of sight," Casey came to his defence.

"Up to a point. Up to a point," the sergeant said. "Everything has its point."

They stopped for tea at the Lawn Hotel in Belturbet. By slipping out to the reception desk while they were eating he managed to pay for the meal. Except for the sergeant's petrol he had paid for the entire day. This was brought up as they parted outside the barracks in the early evening.

"It was a great day. We'll have to make an annual day of the Ulster Final. But next year will be our day. Next year you'll not be allowed to spend a penny," the sergeant said, but still he could see their satisfaction that the whole outing had cost them nothing.

Now that the committal proceedings were at an end an air of uncertainty crept into the dayroom. Did they feel compromised by the day? He did not look at their faces. The door on the river had to be unlocked in order to allow the peace commissioner to leave and was again locked after he left. He caught the sergeant and Guard Casey looking at one another.

"You better show him his place," the sergeant said.

To the right of the door on the river was a big, heavy red door. It was not locked. Casey opened it slowly to show him his cell for the night.

"It's not great, Jimmy, but it's as good as we could get it."

The cement floor was still damp from being washed. Above the cement was a mattress on a low platform of boards. There was a pillow and several heavy grey blankets on the mattress. High in the wall a narrow window was cut, a single steel bar in its centre.

"It's fine. It couldn't be better."

"If you want anything at all, just bang or shout, Jim," and the heavy door was closed and locked. He heard bolts being drawn.

Casually he felt the pillow, the coarse blankets, moved the mattress, and with his palm tested the solidity of the wooden platform; its boards were of white deal and they too had been freshly scrubbed. There was an old oil can beside a steel bucket in the corner. Carefully he moved it under the window, and by climbing on the can and gripping the iron bar he could see out on either side: a sort of lawn, a circular flower-bed, netting-wire, a bole of the sycamore tree, sallies, a strip of river. He tried to get down as silently as possible, but as soon as he took his weight off the oil can it rattled.

"Are you all right there, Jimmy?" Casey was at once asking anxiously from the other side of the door.

"I'm fine. I was just surveying the surroundings. Soon I'll lie down for a while."

He heard Casey hesitate for a moment, but then his feet sounded on the hollow boards of the dayroom, going towards the table and chairs. As much to reassure Casey as from any need, he covered the mattress with one of the grey blankets and lay down, loosening his collar and tie. The bed was hard but not uncomfortable. He lay there, sometimes thinking, more of the time with his mind as blank as the white ceiling, and occasionally he drifted in and out of sleep.

There were things he was grateful for...that his parents were dead...that he did not have to face his mother's uncomprehending distress. He felt little guilt. The share-holders would write him off as a loss against other profits. The old creamery would not cry out with the hurt. People he had always been afraid of hurting, and even when he disliked them he felt that he partly understood them, could put himself in their place, and that was almost the end of dislike. Sure, he had seen evil and around it a stupid, heartless laughing that echoed darkness; and yet, and yet he had wanted to love. He felt that more than ever now, even seeing where he was, to what he had come.

That other darkness, all that surrounded life, used to trouble him once, but he had long given up making anything out of it, like a poor talent, and he no longer cared. Coming into the world, he was sure now, was not unlike getting into this poor cell. There was constant daylight above his head, split by the single bar, and beyond the sycamore leaves a radio aerial disappeared into a high branch. He could make jokes about it, but to make jokes alone was madness. He'd need a crowd for that, a blazing fire, rounds of drinks, and the whole long night awaiting.

There was another fact that struck him now like coldness. In the long juggling act he'd engaged in for years that eventually got him to this cell - four years before only the sudden windfall of a legacy had lifted him clear - whenever he was known to be flush all his loans would flow back as soon as he called; but when he was seen to be in desperate need, nothing worthwhile was ever given back. It was not a pretty picture, but in this cell he was too far out to care much about it now.

He'd had escapes too, enough of them to want no more. The first had been the Roman collar, to hand the pain and the joy of his own life into the keeping of an idea, and to will the idea true. It had been a near thing, especially because his mother had the vocation for him as well; but the pull of sex had been too strong, a dream of one girl in a silken dress among gardens disguising healthy animality. All his life he had moved among disguises, was moving among them still. He had even escaped marriage. The girl he'd loved, with the black head of hair thrown back and the sideways laugh, had been too wise to marry him: no

131

framework could have withstood that second passion for immolation. There was the woman he didn't love that he was resigned to marry when she told him she was pregnant. The weekend she discovered she wasn't they'd gone to the Metropole and danced and drank the whole night away, he celebrating his escape out to where there were lungfuls of air, she celebrating that they were now free to choose to marry and have many children: "It will be no Protestant family." "It will be no family at all." Among so many disguises there was no lack of ironies.

The monies he had given out, the sums that were given back, the larger sums that would never be returned, the rounds of drinks he'd paid for, the names he'd called out, the glow of recognition, his own name shouted to the sky, the day Moon Dancer had won at the Phoenix Park, other days and horses that had lost - all dwindling down to the small, ingratiating act of taking the sergeant and Guard Casey to the Ulster Final.

The bolts were being drawn. Casey was standing in the doorway. "There's something for you to eat, Jimmy." He hadn't realised how dark the cell had been until he came out into the dayroom, and he had to shade his eyes against the light. He thought he'd be eating at the dayroom table, but he was brought up a long hallway to the sergeant's living quarters. At the end of the hallway was a huge kitchen, and one place was set on a big table in its centre. The sergeant wasn't there but his wife was and several children. No one spoke. In the big sideboard mirror he could see most of the room and Casey standing directly behind him with his arms folded. A lovely, strong girl of fourteen or fifteen placed a plate of sausages, black pudding, bacon and a small piece of liver between his knife and fork and poured him a steaming mug of tea. There was brown bread on the table, sugar, milk, salt, pepper. At first no one spoke and his knife and fork were loud on the plate as the children watched him covertly but with intense curiosity. Then Casey began to tease the children about their day in school.

"Thanks," he said after he'd signed a docket at the end of the meal which stated that he had been provided with food.

"For nothing at all," the sergeant's wife answered quietly, but it was little above a whisper, and he had to fight back a wave of gratitude. With Casey he went back down the long hallway to the dayroom. He was moving across the hollow boards to the cell door when Casey stopped him.

"There's no need to go in there yet, Jimmy. You can sit here for a while in front of the fire."

They sat on the yellow chairs in front of the fire. Casey spent a long time arranging turf around the blazing centre of the fire with tongs. There were heavy ledgers on the table at their back. A row of baton cases and the gleaming handcuffs with the green ribbons hung from hooks on the wall. A stripped, narrow bed stood along the wall of the cell, its head beneath the phone on the wall. Only the cell wall stood between Casey's bed and his own plain boards.

"When do you think they'll come?" he asked when the guard seemed to have arranged the sods of turf to his satisfaction.

"They'll come some time in the morning. Do you know I feel badly about all this? It's a pity it had to happen at all." Casey said out of a long silence.

"It's done now anyhow."

"Do you know what I think? There were too many spongers around. They took advantage. It's them that should by rights be in your place."

"I don't know...I don't think so...It was me that allowed it...even abetted it."

"You don't mind me asking this? How did it start? Don't answer if you don't want."

"As far as I know it began in small things. *"He that contemneth small things..."*

"Shall fall little by little into grievous error," Casey finished the quotation in a low, meditative voice as he started to arrange the fire again. "No. I wouldn't go as far as that. That's too hard. You'd think it was God Almighty we were offending. What's an old creamery anyhow? It'll still go on taking in milk, turning out butter. No. Only in law is it anything at all."

"There were a few times I thought I might get out of it," he said slowly. "But the fact is that I didn't. I don't think people can change. They like to imagine they can, that is all."

"Maybe they can if they try hard enough - or they have to," Casey said without much confidence.

"Then it's nearly always too late," he said. "The one thing I feel really badly about is taking the sergeant and yourself to the Ulster Final those few Sundays back. That was dragging the pair of you into the business. That wasn't right."

"The sergeant takes that personally. In my opinion he's wrong. What was personal about it? You gave us a great day out, a day out of all our lives," Casey said. "And everything was normal then."

That was the trouble, everything was not normal then, he was about to say, but decided not to speak. Everything was normal now. He had been afraid of his own fear and was spreading the taint everywhere. Now that what he had feared most had happened he was no longer afraid. His own life seemed to be happening as satisfactorily as if he were free again among people.

Do you think people can change, Ned? He felt like

asking Casey. Do you think people can change or are they given a set star at birth that they have to follow? What part does luck play in the whole shemozzle?

Casey had taken to arranging the fire again and would plainly welcome any conversation, but he found that he did not want to continue. He felt that he knew already as much as he'd ever come to know about these matters. Discussing them further could only be a form of idleness or Clones in some other light. He liked the guard, but he did not want to draw any closer.

Soon he'd have to ask him for leave to go back to his cell.

Wherever You Woke

Dermot Bolger

There only ever was one street,
One back garden, one bedroom:
Wherever you woke, you woke beneath
The ceiling where you were born,
For the briefest unconscious second
An eyelid's flutter from home.

The Outsider

Vincent McDonnell

Philip Moran came in from work. He saw the telegram on the hall table. He picked it up. But he didn't open it. He didn't need to read the message. When he saw the telegram, he knew that his mother was dead.

He wasn't sorry that she was dead. She was a stranger to him now. He hadn't seen her for twenty years. In fact he could hardly remember her. He had no photograph of her. He only had an image of her in his mind. But the years had blurred it.

He had sent her a card on her birthday. He had also sent her a card at Christmas. She had always written to thank him. She always asked him to come home to see her.

"I won't live much longer," she wrote. "I won't see another Christmas." She had written that in every letter. But Philip thought that she would never die. Now she was dead. She wouldn't ask him to come home again.

He went up to his room. It was there he read the telegram. It simply said: Mother is dead. He sat in the

137

battered armchair. He closed his eyes and remembered.

He remembered the day she came to the orphan's home. It was more than thirty years ago. He was only four years old. She brought him a motor car and a bag of sweets. She told him her name was Mary Moran. She said she was taking him home to live with her and her family.

She took him to her own home in the country. There the dog and the hens and the geese frightened him. But it was human beings he learned to fear most.

"You are a lucky lad," the school master said one day. "Your mother is a saint. She took you from the orphan's home. You would still be there if she had not taken you into her home. She treats you like her own son. You owe her everything."

Other people told him he owed her everything. But she herself never asked him for anything.

She treated him as her own son. But other people did not do so. They called him the boarded out boy. His new brothers and sisters called him that too. They were cruel to him.

His brothers punched him. They stood on his toes with their heavy boots. His sister Anna didn't wear heavy boots. She wore light sandals. But he feared her most of all.

He grew afraid of them. He began to dislike them. One day he found that he hated them. He blamed his mother for this. He began to hate her too.

He grew up. At sixteen he left school. At seventeen he went to England. His clothes were packed in an old suitcase. It had a belt around it to keep it closed.

His mother came with him to the train station. She seemed to be an old woman even then. "I'll miss you, Philip," she said.

"You'll soon forget me," he said.

"I won't!" she said. She gripped his hand tightly. There were tears in her eyes.

"I'll come home to visit you," he mumbled. "I'll come for Christmas." But he knew it was a lie. He would never come home again.

"You'll come to my funeral," she said. "I have four sons to carry my coffin. Promise me that you'll come."

He promised that he would come. He boarded the train then. It pulled out from the station. He looked from the window. He saw her for the last time. She was waving goodbye.

In England he rented a room. He got a job on a building site. The work was very hard. He was lonely. But he never went home. He went to the pub every night. He drank and worked and tried to forget his mother.

But he couldn't forget her. So each birthday he sent her a card. Each Christmas he sent her a card. He remembered his last promise to her. He knew that one day a telegram would come. It would tell him that she was dead.

Now that telegram had come. She was dead. He remembered his promise. He would have to go to her funeral. He would have to keep that promise he had made to her the day he left home.

He went back to Ireland. But there was no welcome for him at home. He had not expected any. "You have come too late," his sister Anna said. "She is dead now."

His three brothers shook his hand. They did not speak. They were like three stone statues. But their eyes were sad.

The neighbours shook his hand. They said they were sorry for his trouble. They too were saddened by the death.

They had known his mother all their lives.

He was the only one who wasn't sad. Even when he saw her laid out in the coffin, he wasn't sad. She had loved him. But he hadn't loved her. If he had loved her, wouldn't he feel sorrow now that she was dead?

He looked at her face. It was lined with age. Her hands were joined in prayer. The fingers were like bits of dry sticks. He kissed her forehead. It was cold to his touch.

"You should have let me know that she was sick," he said to Anna.

"You had twenty years," Anna said. "Why didn't you come home then?"

"I didn't know she was sick," he said. "If I knew she was sick I would have come home to see her."

"She didn't want me to send for you," Anna said. "She was afraid you wouldn't come home to see her. It would have broken her heart." He had no answer to that. He knew that he had failed her.

The day of the funeral came. He helped carry her coffin. His brother Martin was on the other side. They had their arms about each other's shoulders. It was the closest they had ever been.

They carried the coffin up the hill to the grave. The priest read the service. They said a decade of the rosary. Then the coffin was lowered into the grave.

Some of the mourners cried. But Philip didn't cry. He felt nothing. He was cold as ice.

Just then a man came up to him. He was quite old, but he looked familiar. "You're Philip, aren't you?" the man said. He shook hands with Philip. "I'm sorry for your trouble," he said.

"Thanks," Philip said.

"I'm Tom Donovan," the man said. "Don't you remember me?"

"I do," Philip said.

"You broke one of my windows when you were a boy."

"Oh yes," Philip said. "I remember that."

"Your mother went quick," Tom said. "I was only talking to her in town last month. She told me she was going to England. She was going to visit you. She had her mind set on it."

"Was she going to England?" Philip asked. He was puzzled.

"She said you had asked her to go over there," Tom said. "She said you were too busy to come home. She said she would have gone many times before but she was afraid of travelling. But she said she was going this time. I was shocked when I heard she was dead."

"I was shocked too," Philip said. "I was expecting her, you see," he lied.

He turned away. He walked down towards the gates. The gravel crunched beneath his shoes. He went through the gates. Then he stopped. He turned around and looked back at the grave. But he still felt nothing.

He had thought that when he saw her dead body he would feel sorrow. But a dead body was only flesh and bone. It would become dust in the grave. You couldn't feel sorrow for dust. You couldn't feel sorrow for bones.

You can't cry for the dead he realised now. You can only cry for what you yourself have lost. If you have lost nothing, you can feel no sorrow.

He remembered now the day he broke Tom Donovan's window. He was more sorry about that. He had been playing football with the lads that day. "I'll kick the ball through the window," he said.

The other lads had laughed at him. They jeered at him. "You're a coward," they had said. "You wouldn't dare."

But he had done it. Even after thirty years or more he could still remember the sound of breaking glass. The boys had yelped in fright. Tom Donovan had come running out of the house. He had shouted at them and shook his fists. They had run away then.

Later that day Tom Donovan had come to the house. He had a stick in his hand. Philip hid in the kitchen.

"Where is Philip?" Tom Donovan had asked. "He broke my window. Now I'm going to break his back with this stick."

"You won't," Philip heard his mother say. "If there's any punishment to be done, I'll see to it myself. No one hits a son of mine."

When Tom went home she had come into the kitchen. She had taken the sally rod down from the mantelpiece. As he had once seen her beat his brothers, now she beat him about the legs. She had beaten him because he, too, was her son.

Now at the graveyard gates he felt the pain again. The rod seemed to be stinging his legs once more. As he felt the pain the years began to turn back like the pages of a book. He began to remember much more of the past.

He remembered the time he had his tonsils out. His throat had been sore. He hadn't been able to sleep at night. He had cried. And each night his mother had come into his bed. She had held him until he slept.

One memory followed another memory. In each memory his mother was alive. These were the memories he had kept hidden. He had hidden them because they could hurt him.

He hadn't wanted to remember her. He hadn't wanted to remember her as she said goodbye. He hadn't wanted to remember the pleading letters she had written. He hadn't wanted to think of her as his mother.

But she had been his mother. She had cared for him. She had cared enough for him to take the rod down from the mantelpiece. She had left welts on the backs of his legs. It had hurt him. But he knew at last that it had hurt her all the more.

Now he emptied himself of his self pity. He began to feel pain again. He began to shake like a tree in the wind. Tears came to his eyes. They ran down his face. He tasted their salt on his lips.

Then his sister Anna was beside him. He saw her face and the tears on her cheeks. He held out his hand to her. She took it in hers and led him back to the car.

The Pattern

Paula Meehan

Little had come down to me of hers,
a sewing machine, a wedding band,
a clutch of photos, the sting of her hand
across my face in one of our wars

when we had grown bitter and apart.
Some say that's the fate of the eldest daughter.
I wish now she'd lasted till after
I'd grown up. We might have made a new start

as women without tags like *mother, wife,*
sister, daughter, taken our chances from there.
At forty-two she headed for god knows where.
I've never gone back to visit her grave.

First she'd scrub the floor with Sunlight soap,
an armreach at a time. When her knees grew sore
she'd break for a cup of tea, then start again
at the door with lavender polish. The smell
would percolate back through the flat to us,
her brood banished to the bedroom.

And as she buffed the wax to a high shine
did she catch her own face coming clear?
Did she net a glimmer of her true self?
Did her mirror tell what mine tells me?
I have her shrug and go on
knowing history has brought her to her knees.

She'd call us in and let us skate around
in our socks. We'd grow solemn as planets
in an intricate orbit about her.

She's bending over crimson cloth,
the younger kids are long in bed.
Late summer, cold enough for a fire,
she works by fading light
to remake an old dress for me.
It's first day back at school tomorrow.

"Pure lambswool. Plenty of wear in it yet.
You know I wore this when I went out with your Da.
I was supposed to be down in a friend's house,
your Granda caught us at the corner.
He dragged me in by the hair- it was long as yours then-
in front of the whole street.
He called your Da every name under the sun,
cornerboy, lout; I needn't tell you
what he called me. He shoved my whole head

under the kitchen tap, took a scrubbing brush
and carbolic soap and in ice-cold water he scrubbed
every spick of lipstick and mascara off my face.
Christ but he was a right tyrant, your Granda.
It'll be over my dead body anyone harms a hair
of your head."

She must have stayed up half the night
to finish the dress. I found it airing at the fire,
three new copybooks on the table and a bright
bronze nib, St. Christopher strung on a silver wire,

as if I were embarking on a perilous journey
to uncharted realms. I wore that dress
with little grace. To me it spelt poverty,
the stigma of the second hand. I grew enough to pass

it on by Christmas to the next in line. I was sizing
up the world beyond our flat patch by patch
daily after school, and fitting each surprising
city street to city square to diamond. I'd watch

the Liffey for hours pulsing to the sea
and the coming and going of ships,
certain that one day it would carry me
to Zanzibar, Bombay, the Land of the Ethiops.

There's a photo of her taken in the Phoenix Park
alone on a bench surrounded by roses
as if she had been born to formal gardens.
She stares out as if unaware
that any human hand held the camera, wrapped
entirely in her own shadow, the world beyond her
already a dream, already lost. She's
eight months pregnant. Her last child.

Her steel needles sparked and clacked,
the only other sound a settling coal
on her sporadic mutter
at a hard part in the pattern.
She favoured sensible shades:
Moss Green, Mustard, Beige.

I dreamt a robe of colour
so pure it became a word.

Sometimes I'd have to kneel
an hour before her by the fire,
a skein around my outstretched hands,
while she rolled wool into balls.
If I swam like a kite too high
amongst the shadows on the ceiling
or flew like a fish in the pools
of pulsing light, she'd reel me firmly
home, she'd land me at her knees.

Tongues of flame in her dark eyes,
she'd say, "One of these days I must
teach you to follow a pattern."

Jack and Annie
Phyl Herbert

Characters.

RITA, a woman in her thirties.

MAISIE, a woman in her forties.

JACK, a man of sixty-five.

ANNIE, Jack's wife, sixty-five.

MS. WHITE, a social welfare official in her twenties.

POLICEMAN, any age.

Setting.

INTERIOR HOUSE SCENES AND STREET SCENES.

Props.

A large map of Ireland, a poster of different cars, ironing board and iron, red earrings, red beret and red silk dress, a few items to suggest dining room and bedroom. Shopping bags.

SCENE 1.

(Two women chatting outside Jack and Annie's house.)

RITA : How are you Maisie?

MAISIE : Exhausted! (Leaving down her shopping bags.) I've just picked up a few things at Dunne's sale.

RITA : I'm staying far away from sales this year. I'm trying to save a few bob for my holidays.

MAISIE : My God! I must be the only one around here that's not plotting something special.

RITA : From now on I'm going to give myself one uplifting treat every year. Life is short Maisie, and I'm determined to break the rut.

MAISIE : (In a confidential tone.) You're not the only one around here who's breaking out.

RITA : What do you mean?

MAISIE : (Looking up at Jack and Annie's bedroom window.) The love birds!

RITA : Jack and Annie. Still in bed. Isn't it great to see them taking advantage of the lie-in.

MAISIE : Twelve o'clock! Wouldn't you think that they would be up at this hour?

RITA : What's their rush? They might as well stay in bed now that he's retired. Don't they deserve the rest?

MAISIE : I'm sure it's rest that pair needs. They're like children with a new toy since they got their free passes, and the old age pension.

RITA : You sound as if you're annoyed with them.

MAISIE : No, I'm not, but you can't claim that he broke his back working.

RITA : He always worked when he got it. It wasn't his fault he never got a permanent job.

MAISIE : I don't know, he was always very choosy.

RITA : Didn't he have a right to be. Anyway they were never short of the few bob.

MAISIE : He always kept the job at the Greyhound Track.

RITA : He also did the odd house-painting job. He got a few bob for that - into his back pocket.

MAISIE : Isn't it strange that he never could bring himself to draw the dole. He was too proud to come down to the level of the rest of us.

RITA : You have to admit that he had a bit of imagination, a bit of style.

MAISIE : Yesterday afternoon the pair of them swanned down the road, hand in hand if you don't mind. She looked absolutely ridiculous.

RITA : Why was that?

MAISIE : Little Red Riding Hood looked pale by comparison. She had a red beret on her and red flashy earrings dangling out of her hair. A peculiar sight if you ask me?

RITA : (Laughing.) More power to her elbow. I love to see a woman dressing up. It's always a sign that there's new life stirring somewhere.

MAISIE : What in the name of God could be new in their lives?

RITA : You can never tell, Maisie.

MAISIE : I don't care what they do but I think they should act their age.

RITA : What has age got to do with it? Are you trying to say that they should lie down and die just because he's getting the pension?

MAISIE : They shouldn't be making fools of themselves, that's all I'm saying.

RITA : Why not? They don't have to set an example to

anybody. Not having children gives them great freedom.

MAISIE : (Dumfounded.) In that case they should consider other peoples' children.

SCENE II.

(Jack and Annie's bedroom. There is a large map of Ireland prominently displayed. Jack is bringing Annie her breakfast in bed.)

JACK : There you are, love. Enjoy your breakfast and don't let the toast get cold.

ANNIE : You have me spoilt, Jack, but I'm not complaining.

JACK : Did you mark your horses?

ANNIE : Yes, "Mr. Frisk" and "Sweet Honey". I'm feeling lucky so put a pound to win on each.

JACK : You'll be ruining my good reputation with all your gambling.

ANNIE : Winning is sweeter than worrying about the neighbours.

JACK : You're right love. I'll be back before lunch. (He goes out.)

ANNIE : (To herself.) This is the life. I don't know what's come over him. This is better than any honeymoon.

(Getting up.) Where did I put those earrings he bought me? He was so pleased when I wore them with the beret. I've never known him to do half the things he's doing now. (She smiles at her reflection in the mirror.) I know one thing for certain, I'm going to enjoy all these treats. (Knock at door...Annie answers door to Ms. White.)

MS. WHITE : Hello, I'm looking for a Mr. Jack Roche, does he live here?

ANNIE : Yes he does. Who are you?

MS. WHITE : I'm Mary White, I'm from the Department of Social Welfare and I need to see him in connection with his pension payments.

ANNIE : He's out at the moment but he'll be back shortly. Would you like to come in and wait for him?

MS. WHITE : Thanks very much. I just want him to fill in a few details.

ANNIE : Oh! (Looking surprised.)

MS. WHITE : Just routine.

ANNIE : Would you like a cup of tea while you're waiting?

MS. WHITE : That would be lovely, Mrs. Roche. (Annie prepares tea while Ms. White snoops around the room.) I'm admiring your T.V. and Video set. They must be the very latest models.

ANNIE : Yes, that's right, aren't they beautiful! Jack bought them for me. He's been showering me with gifts ever since he got the pension.

MS. WHITE : Is that so? (Enquiringly.)

ANNIE : These past few weeks have been like one long holiday. We've had a celebration almost every day.

MS. WHITE : I see. (Sarcastically.) (Noises outside.)

ANNIE : That'll be Jack. (Jack enters.)

ANNIE : Jack, this is Miss White. She is from the Department of Social Welfare and she wants you to answer some questions.

JACK : I thought I was finished with all that.

MS. WHITE : This won't take long, Mr. Roche. I have to ask you a few questions to ascertain the rate of your pension. You could call it a Means Test.

JACK : What exactly are you on about?

MS. WHITE : I'm sure you are aware that your pension is Non-Contributory due to the fact that you were not employed long enough with any one employer to earn a Contributory Pension.

JACK : I'm well aware of that. I know the State is paying my pension.

MS. WHITE : Good. It is my job to satisfy the Department that the household is dependent on your pension.

JACK : Of course it is. My wife doesn't work and I have no other source of income.

MS. WHITE : (Looking around the room.) You're doing a grand job, Mr. Roche. The house is looking good on a single income.

JACK : (Defensively.) Why wouldn't it? Anything wrong with that? Are you disappointed that we have the normal items that every house in the neighbourhood has?

MS. WHITE : Do you mean every house around here has the very latest T.V. and Video? I must be missing out somewhere!

JACK : That one is not ours. We are minding it for a friend who is away for a while. Break-ins are common around here.

MS. WHITE : (Looking at Annie.) I have established that there is no other income besides your pension. Would you sign here Mr. Roche?

JACK : Would you like it in blood?

MS. WHITE : Thank you, Mr. Roche. You'll be hearing from the Department in due course.

ANNIE : I'll see you out Miss White.

JACK : The bitch, how dare she pry into what we have in our home. You'd think my pension was coming out of her pocket.

ANNIE : I wouldn't mind if you never got a penny from them. You know Jack it's an awful pity you were so proud.

JACK : I feel like a fish that was filleted in its own water. What do they expect to find? I suppose they'd be happy to find us eating porridge. God, that attitude makes me sick!

ANNIE : Now love don't get upset.

JACK : (Smirking.) I wasn't going to tell her that I bought the video out of our win.

ANNIE : I suppose she's only doing her job.

JACK : How come nobody else around here is Means Tested for the pension?

ANNIE : They were Means Tested for the Labour years ago and the Department never comes back to bother them.

JACK : So I'm the new fish in their net. If they interfere with my pension, Annie I won't be responsible for what I do.

ANNIE : Relax, Jack. I'll get something to eat. (Prepares lunch.) Did you meet anybody at the shops?

JACK : I met Maisie. She's a nosey streak of misery. She wanted to know why we weren't down at the pub lately.

ANNIE : What did you tell her?

JACK : I made up some cock and bull story.

ANNIE : That woman thinks we owe her an explanation for breathing the same air as she does.

JACK : Spare me, O Lord from miserable minds. (Changing mood.) Close your eyes and hold out your hands.

(He places a small parcel in her hands)

ANNIE : (Opening present.) Lipstick....(She puts it on.) Jack are you trying to make a scarlet woman out of me? (She kisses him.) Thank you my sweet.

SCENE III.

(Rita and Maisie meet one week later at the Supermarket.)

MAISIE : Good morning, Rita.

RITA : Good morning, Maisie.

MAISIE : (Exhausted.) I didn't sleep a wink last night with the noise coming from Jack and Annie's house.

RITA : It's not like them to be noisy.

MAISIE : True. But there is something peculiar going on. They arrived home last night very late and their roars of laughter woke me up. I couldn't believe my ears.

RITA : I take it they were highly amused at something.

MAISIE : At their age what could cause such hilarity?

RITA : They say at each phase of life there is a new discovery!

MAISIE : At their age they should be saying their prayers. It can't be good for their hearts to be getting that excited.

RITA : I envy them anyway. No children to hold them back.

MAISIE : If I didn't have my kids I'd have nothing.

RITA : I don't know about that. Children stop you doing a lot of things.

MAISIE : Like what?

RITA : When I was a teenager I could always see myself doing all sorts of exotic things when I started working.

MAISIE : What, for instance?

RITA : I always had a dream about riding horses and travelling around the country to different race meetings and becoming the best jockey in Ireland.

MAISIE : You're mad, I never wanted to do anything else except get married and have children.

RITA : Are you happy now that you've achieved that?

MAISIE : You must be joking!

RITA : Maisie, I think you should take a little holiday. Go off for a week-end by yourself and leave the lot of them behind.

MAISIE : My shower wouldn't be able to cope without me.

RITA : I don't think they'd starve. There's no point in being a martyr.

MAISIE : (Smiling.) Maybe I should take a page from Jack and Annie's book.

SCENE IV.

(Jack and Annie's house. In addition to the map of Ireland there is displayed a large poster of different car models. Jack is returning from his daily rounds of shopping and betting. Annie is ironing a red silk dress.)

JACK : My God! People are terrible begrudgers.

ANNIE : What's the matter, Jack? Are you alright?

JACK : I wish that crowd of kids would mind their own business.

ANNIE : Maisie's kids again. They have absolutely no manners on them. What did they say this time?

JACK : Ah! Something about Bonnie and Clyde and....(He hesitates.) What does it matter?

ANNIE : You're right Jack. Their parents are madly jealous.

JACK : If they won the lotto they wouldn't know how to spend it. They deserve their misery. What am I wasting my breath on them for? Come here to me my sweet, Annie.

ANNIE : Yes, my love.

JACK : (Taking down map from wall.) Where would madam like to visit today?

ANNIE : (Studying map.) I think we should stick with the west coast. (Teasing Jack.) We've started so we'll finish. Galway, Jack, the city of the Tribes and of the Claddagh. I've always wanted to see Galway before I died.

JACK : Then so be it. Galway it will be. (Taking down poster of cars from the wall.) What style car would madam wish to travel in?

ANNIE : I'll leave that up to you, Jack.

JACK : Can you remember what we used for Cork?

ANNIE : Of course I can. Do you think I'm a dumb blonde? It was a Volvo. Smooth as a bird in flight.

JACK : Right on, Annie! Volvo is my favourite. I can't say the same for the other car. She was a bit tricky on the old gears. We were lucky to make Cork in one piece.

ANNIE : (Excited.) What will it be for Galway?

JACK : Take your pick - Jaguar, Mercedes, Porsche.

ANNIE : (Hesitant.) Do you really think we should risk another car?

JACK : Mustn't weaken, Annie, we never got anything out of them up to now. We have to take what we want-before it's too late.

ANNIE : But we still have the free travel.

JACK : Yes, but I have to prove my point. Now back to cars. (Holding Annie's hands.) Love of my life, I would over-power the lock on any car in this city for my Annie.

SCENE V.

(The street. Ms. White knocks on Maisie's Door.)

MS. WHITE : Hello, I'm sorry to disturb you but I'm trying to contact Mr. Jack Roche.

MAISIE : He lives next door.

MS. WHITE : Yes, I know, but I've tried calling and there is no answer. In fact, this is my third visit this week.

MAISIE : I haven't laid eyes on them for a while now. I'm beginning to be concerned.

MS. WHITE : Why would you be concerned?

MAISIE : They have been behaving very curiously of late. You would never know what they're up to.

MS. WHITE : Oh! Is that so? In what way have they been behaving curiously?

MAISIE : They're ridiculous. They get dressed up every day and trot off hand-in-hand to explore the country.

MS. WHITE : A romantic couple, would you say?

MAISIE : I would if they were forty years younger, but that sort of lovey dovey when you're over forty is not on.

MS. WHITE : Why not?

MAISIE : (Flustered.) Come on now....By the way I don't know who you are. Are you a relative?

MS WHITE : No, I'm afraid not. My name is Mary White. I'm from the Department of Social Welfare.

MAISIE : In that case I'll say goodbye.

SCENE VI.

(The street. Rita calling to Maisie.)

MAISIE : How are you Rita?

RITA : I'm alright, but I can't relax.

MAISIE : Why not?

RITA : I can't get that image out of my head. The sight of seeing Jack and Annie walking around the car park in Kildare Street.

MAISIE : Are you quite sure it was them?

RITA : Positive, but when I said 'hello' they turned away.

MAISIE : What on earth would they be doing in a car park in Kildare Street?

RITA : Isn't that where the Government Ministers work?

MAISIE : I believe so!

RITA : What do you think their interest was in walking around a car park?

MAISIE : It doesn't bear thinking about. Do you think they might have gone senile?

RITA : Not at all, Maisie, people don't become senile overnight.

MAISIE : I suppose not, I think you slow down with senility and that has not happened in their case.

RITA : Do you think we should have a look around their house, see if we can spot anything?

MAISIE : I've already got the children to look in the back window but perhaps we should have another look.

SCENE VII

(Outside Jack and Annie's House. Maisie and Rita discover Ms. White with a policeman.)

MAISIE : Mother of God, they're not dead are they?

POLICEMAN : No, but I have their permission to collect some of their possessions.

RITA : Are they alright? Where are they?

MS. WHITE : They are in a hospital in Galway but they are in no danger, healthwise.

MAISIE : What is the policeman doing here?

MS. WHITE : Well that is another story.

RITA : Please tell us what this is all about.

MS. WHITE : Mr. and Mrs. Roche were involved in a car crash in Galway.

MAISIE : Did some car knock them down?

MS. WHITE : No, they were the ones doing the knocking.

MAISIE : What do you mean?

MS. WHITE : Mr. Roche was the driver, and he drove into the side of a shop in Galway.

RITA : But I didn't know he drove.

MAISIE : There must be some mistake because they had no car, they always used their free travel passes.

MS. WHITE : They must have been giving the free passes a rest, because the car they were found in was driven by them from Dublin.

RITA : Why would they want to drive when they can get the train free?

MS. WHITE : It's a mystery to me.

MAISIE : Did they hire the car or what?

MS. WHITE : That is the most absurd part of the story. The car was stolen.

MAISIE : Stolen, they hired a stolen car?

MS. WHITE : No, they stole the car and apparently it was not the first car they stole.

RITA : Maybe they are going senile after all!

POLICEMAN : No, I'm afraid not, Mr. Roche made a statement to the effect that what he did was a deliberate act. He admitted stealing the car. The speed at which that Peugeot was driven must have been a rare sight around Galway Bay. It is reported that when the Galway Police gave chase they thought that Nigel Mansell must have been giving the Peugeot a test run. They might never have been caught if they hadn't hit that shop on the corner.

MAISIE : Are they going to be charged for this?

POLICEMAN : Yes, they will be charged with Joyriding and damage to property.

MAISIE : Joyriding, joyriders. How on earth will I explain that to the kids?

RITA : Thank God they're safe, anyway.

For Joan
John McArdle

Author's note: I wrote this poem for my daughter, Joan, on her last birthday before she got married to Odhran. It is about the way life and love go on through our children to our children's children.

Once you wrote me a poem on my birthday
About fixing wonky wheels I'd wonked myself,
Carrying you upside-down to bed,
Teaching you to say
 "Daddy, when I was younger ---"
Because you were too young for
 "Daddy, when I was young --"
When you wrote it you were sixteen and big --- bigger,
The biggest you'd ever been up to that.
Now you are big enough to leave,
Too big for the wicker chair
And this is the last birthday before you grow more.
We're spreading wings faster than before.
The farthest. On birthdays now we don't light flares,
Drink coke, eat cake, go wild.
Birthdays are becoming, not mild, but milder affairs.

By next birthday Odhran will be writing the poem,
Replacing the love that teaches with the love that shares
And then, maybe, fixes wonky things and teaches again
To know the world of wheels and mice and men.

The Market Road

David McCart-Martin

It was a long climb up from the island. Really it was a peninsula, joined to the mainland by a curving, sloping road, holed and pitted. Away to one side a large hill, mound-shaped, rose steeply. On the opposite side the road stopped at a small, uneven bank, beyond which lay marsh and shallows. Among other night sounds John could hear the tinkling of the wind breaking the surface of the pools. It was now blowing directly up the narrow lough as it changed round to the north and east, a much colder wind.

The horse was snorting heavily as it pulled the creaking cart towards the point where the island road joined the main road. The moon was high and brilliant, only occasionally becoming hidden by a cluster of cloud; it made the autumn landscape seem harsh, spectral. The shallows, mirroring it in a cold white light, made the shadows sharp-edged and the progression of horse, cart and man seem almost non-existent.

He was walking beside the horse now, talking softly

to it, rubbing its neck with a piece of rough cloth as it strained towards the summit. He watched the boxes and crates on the back jostle and knock against one another as the wheels of the cart creaked through the ruts, stopping to go round, pulling and testing the ropes which held them in place. Gaining the top, the horse wheeled onto the main road and halted at his soft, quick word. He kept talking to it as he wiped its shiny neck and shoulders, feeling its muzzle snuffling among the oats in his hand. The wind was rising, biting with a keener edge. Throwing a piece of sacking across the horse's back he paused, listening to its breathing becoming normal, and the moaning of the wind increase. His eyes were fixed on the dusky blob of the island. Pinpricks of light were grouped here and there like glow worms in a bush. Others, isolated, blinked faintly like remote stars.

His eyes held one, the dully glinting spark transformed within his own mind. She would be by the fire, a garment in her lap as she sewed, at times turning her eyes towards the window where the lamp shone even though she knew he wouldn't return until the next afternoon. The dog would be lying in a corner at the door, its ears pricking as the wind changed quarter, sensitive to its unaccustomed bed. Usually the dog slept in an outhouse but, upon John's insistence, was here nights he had to be away. She would rather he took the dog with him, for companionship, if nothing else. But no, traditions as old as the island and its cold sea winds instinctively told him of the rights of protector and protected.

Momentarily he leaned against the horse. His vision was beginning to blur, though his eyes still held the flicker of light. He moved, his hand stroking his thigh, as if he could indeed feel her warm softness against his own flesh. Over the ridge of the island the north channel was a cold smooth paleness where the landmass of Scotland loomed bulkily towards him. The brightness of the moon made the sea a river and cast into prominence the great dome of Ailsa Craig adrift on the water.

Turning abruptly, he clucked the horse into a measured walking pace, walking himself for several hundred yards and feeling the warmth flowing into his limbs. Jumping up onto the cart he found his place, wedging himself between two bales after pulling another thick coat around his shoulders. The peaked cap was pulled low across the broad forehead and thick eyebrows. A match flared as he sucked on a pipe, the bowl suddenly hot in his hand.

It was a long road to the market in the city. Leaving well before midnight he would arrive sometime after an autumn dawn. The selling and buying would come first, and then the other odd items of business would be done over pints of porter and a meal much interspaced by yarns and tales to be carried home as news. Heavy with food and sleep, a few hours' doze was to be had in front of the big open range of the public house, then back on the cart again for the journey home.

His sight was keen to the road, his hearing too. It opened in front of him, folding round bends he knew intimately. Sometimes he looked behind him, sometimes at the sky where the moon was swiftly traversing its brilliant passage. The soft swishing of the wind in the hedgerows fell to his ears and, twice, the bark of a fox. But gradually the rhythmic beat of hoofs on the roadway and the measured creaking of the cart began to displace all else. The slight rocking sensation felt reassuring, it eased his cramped limbs. The slight tingling pressure was there again in his thigh, testimony to the soft warmth of her flesh. The lamp, too, but more dimly now, shone in the warm room beneath the thatch while outside the cold sea winds chuckled in the eaves.

He was almost on the ground before his senses were

sharp again. The horse reared between the shafts, its loud neighing cracking open the silence of the road. The reins sailed over its back where they had been tugged violently from his hands. Swiftly he regained his balance and ran up to grasp the halter, one hand stroking the horse's neck, his eyes simultaneously taking in the shadows and the arching line of trees on either side which, had they been in bloom, would have blotted out the sky. The horse reared again and, turning quickly, he crooked his arm to shield his head from the blow, trying to restrain his sudden surge of fear. None came. Again he grasped the halter, his eyes searching, seeing nothing.

Sweat itched on his scalp. "Woa, girl, woa. Steady now, steady does it. Hold there, hold a bit." His voice was sharp, urgent. Turning quickly again he pulled at the horse, one hand running from its shoulder to the belly, his sharp rush of words battling with its terror for control.

It was then he saw it. Half-hidden by the bales, it lay along the back of the cart, front paws drooping over the side. Its head turned towards him and large dark eyes watched him passively. He tried to suck back the laughter as it burst out in a sudden exclamation of relief. The dog didn't stir. Quietening the horse he began to call to it, whistling and cracking his fingers. But still the dog didn't move.

Cursing softly, more at the receding vestiges of his own hysteria, he looped the reins around a shaft and walked towards the rear. At his movement the dog dropped onto the road and made away in a long, loping stride, stopping when he stopped, moving on when he moved. He attempted to approach it for a last time and then stood still, simply watching. It was a massive beast, heavy-shouldered, its coat seemingly a reddish-brown. Thick fangs glinted over a lolling tongue. Back at the cart he paused for several moments to watch the dull shape in the middle of the road which seemed to be coming imperceptibly closer.

When the horse reared again he knew that their strange companion had returned. Immediately he was on the ground, one hand clutching her mane, talking, clucking his tongue. She soon became quiet, though she still trembled. Again he turned to find the great head with its dark eyes watching him silently. It lay as before. He stood, puzzling, his mind sifting among half-a-lifetime's experience of the land and beasts. Once more he tried to get near it, but to no avail. It kept just ahead of him and, when he stopped, stopped also to turn and watch.

"It's a quare strange one, right enough," he mused to the horse as the cart jolted into motion, smiling at his own chagrin. Fatigue was now getting the better of him and there was still a fair way to go. And there'd been the good part of an hour lost, which meant a late start for the journey home. He forced his eyes on the horse's every movement as she plodded ahead of him and, within a short time, was rewarded by a snort as she tried to turn, her rump hitting a shaft. But this time he quietened her as she kept moving, and soon she was walking steadily, as if having accepted his confidence that here was no harm. Glancing over his shoulder he saw the dog in the same position, though now its eyes were turned on the shadows at the side of the road. He regained his former place, the bales taking the weight of his back.

They broke into open countryside, leaving the avenue of trees behind. A sudden intuition made him look sideways, and he saw that the dog had left the cart. It paused to look at him, then vanished over a bank. Several times he involuntarily turned, but saw nothing. Shrugging his shoulders he pulled the coat more tightly round his body, noting with quiet anticipation the first fingers of dawn streak the eastern sky. Soon there would be food and warmth.

By mid-afternoon he'd finished his business. The cart was empty, save for four young turkeys in a crate, their beaks sticking out between the slats. He sat before the range of the pub, replete with porter and stew, his few other purchases on the floor beside him. Some tools, tobacco, yarn, a present of perfume and a scarf for her. Rousing himself with difficulty he went outside and harnessed the horse, his mind still buzzing with the talk and laughter, the hard bartering, of the past few hours. The wind was higher and more bitter, but a clear sky promised that the night would be otherwise fine. He was even later in starting than he'd imagined, and would be long overdue in reaching the island.

They were waiting for him in the yard. Turning down the narrow track which led to the farmhouse he saw the lanterns, and wondered. As he wheeled the horse towards the barn the group of neighbours came towards him. She was among them. A big woman, the heavy coat across her shoulders increased a sense of masculinity about her character. Her voice was high, anxious. "Thank God, it's you, John. You're late this night. We thought..."

He jumped down and began unharnessing the horse, slow to reply. "Aye, I'm late. But it's not the first time I've been late from the market."

They pressed closer, their lanterns swinging. "Did ye see anythin' on the market road, John?" a neighbour asked.

He started rubbing the horse down. "Not a thing," he said. "I didn't see a thing."

Another voice spoke, but softer. "It was Tim McCalmont, John. That started out less than an hour after ye."

He paused to look at the speaker, keen to the other's tone. "And what about Tim McCalmont?"

"He's dead. It was a sorry sight, I'm telling ye. They

cut his throat and him hardly twenty pound in his pocket. Don't ye know the long mile?"

"I do," he said, thinking of the long straight part of the road where the trees bent overhead and hugged innumerable shadows between them.

"It was there we found him. Lyin' beside his cart."

"A sorry sight he was," another echoed. "And murdered for hardly twenty pound in his pocket."

In the bright splash of a lantern he saw the mongrel bitch squeeze between the legs of the men. Forgotten, the incident of the previous night passed swiftly through his mind and he shivered. He saw himself turning, bending, one hand on the horse, the other shielding his head from a blow that didn't come. And the great dog that lay along the back of the cart, watching him passively. Abruptly he turned the horse and started walking towards the barn, the bitch in attendance at his heels, going now to her usual bed.

"An' ye're sure ye didn't see anythin', John?"

His voice was harsh as he called over his shoulder. "I'm tellin' ye I didn't see a thing! I didn't see a thing on the market road 'cept a dog."

Slippery Slopes

Declan Collinge

On winter nights
When frost had sugared
Hedge tops and blanched
The avenues to sparkling
Brilliance, we laced
Our driveway slopes
With water, which froze
To black ice overnight.

Then, with patient polishing
We honed our slopes
To an ice-rink surface
Lining up with strident calls
To run and slide,
Legs splayed, arms extended
With young abandon.

Housewives fearing for
Life and limb
Scattered salt
To gap our slides
Curtailing rapid movement
Prematurely halting games
Before the midday sun.

I feel the pang of frost
In my joints
A black ice seizes
My thought as twilight
Brings the frozen sky
To sparkling brilliance
I walk briskly
To warm my blood
Mindful of winter
Fearful of slippery slopes.

The Poacher

(from Hell Hath No Fury)
Malcolm MacDonald

Trapper knew that Two-horses Flynn continued to take rabbits, despite several convictions for poaching. Last time the RM had warned him that the next conviction would earn him a spell "up the Cut" - not his words, of course, but the local term for going to jail. Far from discouraging Flynn, the warning had simply made him more cautious. "There's no sleeping it out with *me*," he boasted in his favourite bars. "They'll have to stir themselves nice and early to make good that oul' threat."

Trapper took the man at his word. He was out at Flynn's well before dawn, wrapped up warm in an old coachman's coat, fortified with a nip of good brandy, and cradling his trusty double-barrelled shotgun across his knees. He had chosen a place where a gap in the wall gave rabbits easy passage between the two properties. If he were Flynn, that is where he would set his traps - and remove them before sun-up, too.

He chose well, for he had not been there ten minutes before he heard the sudden snap of the iron jaws and the terrified shriek of an animal in pain. A rabbit, beyond doubt, a large buck by the sound of him. Flynn's tigeen was half a mile away, but he'd surely hear the racket, Trapper thought. Twenty minutes later he heard the man himself approaching. What annoyed Trapper most of all was that the trap had been laid on the Coolderg side of the wall; the fellow wasn't even poaching his own land! Still, it provided all the more excuse for blasting away.

Trapper had chosen a range that would give Flynn a nasty peppering - maybe blind him in one eye with luck - but not one that would risk his life. It would be enough of a warning to him, and everyone else, that nobody insulted and stole from the Lyndon-Furys and got away with it.

Trapper smiled to himself. The RIC and the judiciary were all very well in their way. But for seven hundred years the English had been teaching the Irish that it was both honourable and patriotic to break the law; they had it blunted as a weapon of 'natural justice', which now lay, instead, in the arsonist's torch, the hamstringer's knife, the bullet in the mails.

The first light of false dawn laid a faint and bleary finger of pink upon the skyline as Trapper raised the shotgun to his shoulder. The light was just sufficient to show the movement of the man as he came to the gap in the wall. The rabbit was still screaming.

Perhaps its racket drowned out Trapper's warning cry of "Poacher! Halt or I fire!" Flynn certainly took no evasive action.

Trapper aimed off about fifteen degrees and let him have one barrel.

For a moment there was utter silence. Then the rabbit started screaming again. Of Flynn there was no sign.

Trapper leaped to his feet and finished the creature off with the toe of his boot, throwing it well into the Coolderg demesne before turning his mind to the hunt for Flynn. The man would surely have made for the lough shore, he reasoned.

But then, from a hundred yards off in the opposite direction - towards the muddy creek between Flynn's peninsula and the rest of the country - came a taunting laugh. "You missed me, your honour, sir. Missed by a mile!"

It wasn't true, in fact. Five or six pellets had found their mark and were causing Two-horses slight discomfort, but he wasn't going to give Trapper Lyndon-Fury the satisfaction of knowing it. As soon as he had delivered his taunt he turned and set off like the wind for the open country beyond the creek. When he reached the edge, he paused long enough to be sure Trapper was following him; then, picking his way safely through the mire, he hopped and lepped to safety.

Trapper had less luck. Halfway over the creek he slithered in the ooze, caught his ankle in an old waterlogged tree trunk that lay half in and half out of the mud, and pitched headlong. The gun went skittering before him and lodged in the branches of the fallen tree. Cursing like a demon he tried to rise but all he did was slither into deeper water. He gathered his legs beneath him for a spring back to the firmer shallows, only to feel the bed yield at the pressure. Then his boots sank into a bottomless space that was filled with something that felt like half-melted butter. After that, every struggle seemed to suck him deeper into the cloying mass.

"Flynn, damn your eyes!" he cried out. "Come and help me, confound you."

Flynn paused in his flight and listened.

"I'm stuck," came the distant cry.

Smiling to himself he crept back as silent as a shade; it could be a trap, of course.

"Over here!" The cry was more pleading now.

He sought the protection of a stout sally and called out, "Has yer honour any sort of a landmark at all?"

"Can't see a bloody thing. I was tripped up by some kind of waterlogged tree on its side."

That confirmed it. The man was stuck. This was no trap. "Would your honour have the goodness and patience to wait till I fetch a lantern and a length of rope?" he asked.

"Devil take you!" Trapper called back. "I'll freeze to death while you're gone. Just find an old branch or something and throw it to me. I'm damned sure I could get myself out if only...Flynn?" He heard the sounds of the man's departure, which Flynn no longer bothered to conceal. "God's curse on you!" he called after him bitterly.

"And the divil bless your honour, too!" was the murmured reply.

Flynn took his time about it - enough, indeed, to brew a cup of tea. He poured it lovingly and helped it stand up with a hint of something stronger. He drained the dark, sweet mixture with relish and set off in search of rope and lantern.

It was a good half hour before he arrived back at the creek. By now the true dawn was almost strong enough to let him do without the lantern; but its light would help, he thought, to bring out the finer details of Lyndon-Fury's expression. He wanted to see the man's anger - to have something to treasure during the long winter evenings ahead.

"Christ but you took your time," Trapper cried angrily as he saw the approaching lantern.

"Sure there's nothing worse than a piece of rope

that'd part company with itself at the first pull."

"Throw it here, man, and stop your blather." Trapper held out an impatient hand.

Flynn spotted the gun, which had come to rest in the bough of the tree. "Jesus, Mary, and Joseph!" he cackled. "Isn't that a sight for two sore eyes!"

He broke the gun and took out the cartridge, which he popped in his pocket with a grin. "I'll save yer honour the postage, so," he explained cheerily.

"Fuck you, Flynn! I'll see the colour of your brains if I have to use the butt. And you needn't think this is the end of the affair, either. I'll hound you and your cronies to the gates of hell. A dying dog wouldn't change places with you before I'm done - so you may wipe that stupid grin off your face this instant. And give me that fucking rope!" He held out his hand with the assurance of one whose word was law.

The grin, stupid or not, vanished from the other's lips. Trapper's words had painted a sudden picture of his life over the next weeks or months. The police would watch his every move; his every petty trespass would be stamped upon with all the majesty of the law. Their law. Let his horse shy at an oul' sack blowing in the ditch and he'd be up in court for reckless driving. Let the wind knock the legs from under him and he'd get three days for drunk and disorderly.

Blind rage possessed him, helped, no doubt, by the poteen. He'd never be free of their persecution. And who was it said that while one Irishman remained unfree, Ireland herself was still in chains. Wasn't that as good as saying when one Irishman liberated himself from his own bondage, he struck a blow for the whole nation?

He turned and stared at the gun.

No! screamed every cautious fibre in his body.

Yes! urged an anger that had grown fat down the centuries of persecution and injustice.

Slowly his fingers snaked into the pocket where they had popped the cartridge only moments earlier.

The fatal wound was convenient to Trapper's left eye. Sergeant McNair of the RIC saw at once what had happened. Trapper, who, as all the world knew, was his own gamekeeper, had caught Flynn poaching rabbits and had given him a mild taste of one of the barrels. Flynn, of course, said he was out pulling thorns into the gaps where the cattle might stray - before dawn, indeed! But it was obvious he'd been poaching. The dead rabbit with its legs all torn proved it. And the muddy footprints beyond the creek showed which way the ragged rascal had run, and how Trapper had followed him - with the gun unbroken and the fatal cartridge still loaded. Once he blundered into that fallen tree in the dark, the rest had followed as night follows day.

By the time the sergeant had it all neatly pieced together, it was so convincing that Flynn had to remind himself that *he* was the real hero of the action.

St. Vincent's Night Shelter, Backlane, Dublin

Pádraig J. Daly

Winter nearly here,
The extra beds are out
In Back Lane Hostel.

There are lumps of good
Beef in the stew,
The pipes give heat
Like the softly burning
Turnip God's Son's
Statue has
For a heart.

The smell of drink
And thawing feet
Fills the big room,
We sit around, shirts
Are washed
For a new morning,
Cigarettes are rolled.

One man takes a tin flute
From his pocket

And in a corner near
Misery plays old Hope
Back in, whiteshirted,
Smelling of soap.

Sweetie Pie
Miriam Gallagher

Tom didn't come home last night. I don't care. And let me tell you something for nothing. I don't mind if he never comes home again. And I mean that.

You see it wasn't so much what he was doing. I mean to say we all have to make a living don't we? And it's hard making a living in New York. No, it wasn't that, but how often. God, I sound like the priest in confession.

"How often did you do it?"

I can hardly bring myself to tell anyone about it. When they asked me to write it all down, I thought of you and how I could always tell you things and you wouldn't laugh like the others. So I'm writing it down. All of it.

And when I've finished maybe they'll let me go. After all I did nothing.

All the time I did nothing. I mean I'm not the one that has to go to confession. He is. So I don't have to worry about a thing. I don't need to be afraid. After all I did nothing.

When I met Tom at the Pizza Place on First Avenue, I thought he was the best thing that could ever happen to me. I loved the way he pushed his black curly hair out of his eyes and his slow lazy smile. I suppose I am a bit childish in a way, but that was because my mother always kept us under lock and key. Not in any cruel way mind. Just to keep us out of harm's way. Or so she said.

Maybe when I've written it all down exactly how it was they'll let me go and I'll cross the street to the Pizza Place on First Avenue. I'll buy a slice with pepperoni and get a can of diet Pepsi. I want to keep my figure nice. Men like you when you look nice. No one knows that better than me. I'll sit at a table near the door. Maybe when the wind blows the papers in through the café doorway I'll look up to see who has come in. It could be Tom. And maybe I'll tell him then. Maybe.

He was full of surprises, often coming home when I didn't expect him. It was the work he did I suppose. But I never asked. That was one of the ways he got around me.

Surprise. I used to love the little surprises he gave me when we were together at the start.

One evening he came home with a fur coat. And it was for me. Now if that happened to my mother she'd throw a fit and think that the coat was stolen. But I knew better. I know what men are like. Not like my mother. She never had a clue. So when Tom came home and looked at me with that light in his eyes I knew there was something up. I mean a nice surprise. I shut my eyes as he asked me to and when he put the soft fur up to my neck. I smiled and turned to kiss him.

"So who's my Sweetie Pie then?" he asked.

I didn't answer except with my eyes and he knew then I was his Sweetie Pie and not going off with another.

I asked no questions. And we were happy. My

mother always told me not to keep on asking people things because sometimes they don't know the answer and you only make them feel uneasy. So I never asked him anything. And that was just the way he liked it. He told me so often there could be no doubt about that.

When he brought me home nice surprises I kissed him and he was happy. I'd have kissed him anyway but he seemed to think that I'd fall for him more than ever if he gave me things. Oh now, don't get me wrong. I love a fur coat as well as the next woman. Don't we all?

At the start I loved him bringing me things. Anything at all. Well, that was at the start. I mean when a girl gets a fur coat as a surprise it's hard to give her a better surprise than that.

Then Tom got it wrong. Not that he could help it. It really wasn't his fault. You see he thought that just because I kissed him like I did when he brought me the coat, that was my heart's desire. Dear God, if he only knew! I never liked the idea of animals being killed just so as you and me could go out all dolled up in their skins. But for the sake of peace I let on to him that I loved the coat. And in a way I did. Well at least I did the first time. And a couple of times after that. But when he kept on bringing me fur coats, I knew what to expect. I mean a surprise is not a surprise if you know what it is.

That was when I made my first mistake. I told him. He wasn't pleased. He wasn't pleased at all. He stopped kissing me and looked at me with a hard look, the kind of look I'd seen him give the men on First Avenue when they tried to stop him for a light for their cigarette. At least I think that's what they wanted.

"So my little Sweetie Pie doesn't want a nice surprise then?"

"No." I bit my lip. "I mean it's lovely Tom, really it is,

but-"

"But what?" He held me by the hair. I didn't move a muscle. "Come on, tell dear old Tom what it is, Honey." He tugged my hair so that it hurt.

I began to cry. I didn't mean to. It just happened. You see men always like me and no one ever did that to me before. But when I tried to tell him I couldn't get the words out because I was sobbing. That made him angry. Tom doesn't like it if you cry. Most men don't. My mother always told me, cry yourself if you must but don't let on to a man that you're full of tears because that makes them feel uneasy. Well I couldn't help it. You know what I'm like. A real softie. If I see someone on the telly in a car crash I nearly pass out with the horror. It's like it was happening to me and I cry. But only when I'm on my own. Once or twice I almost let Tom see me cry by mistake but managed to slip out to make tea and get him a drink before he saw the worst of my tears. One time a little child was dying on the telly and his mother couldn't save him. They were out in Africa or somewhere with a lot of strange animals and in danger. I couldn't get that little child out of my mind for a long while. Other people must be very brave all the time not to cry. My mother said everyone cries sometimes but they never let on. It only makes people uneasy and gives them the idea that you are a softie. Which I am. And I agreed with her but in my heart I wondered why you couldn't let the tears fall and why you had to keep them inside you or else rush off into a secret place to weep.

That day when he saw me crying Tom let go of my hair and ran out of the room. Then I let all the tears that were inside me flow like a waterfall. They made the fur coat all wet and looking like a cat that had washed itself. I put it on a hanger beside the other fur coats and turned the part that was wet with tears towards the wall so he wouldn't notice.

Then I had an idea. As I looked at all the coats hanging there I thought to myself this is crazy. I don't need them. So why keep them? I thought of all the people on First Avenue who'd give their eye teeth for one. So I picked out my favourite. It was the first one he gave me and if I tell the truth the only one that was a real surprise. All the other times I was letting on to him that I was thrilled when I wasn't.

I put my favourite to one side and put all the others into a plastic bag and crept down the stairs. He didn't hear me. But that didn't surprise me. Once he has a little drink he goes all quiet and dozes off. I forgot to say about his drinking. But then they said tell us everything even if it seems silly.

When I got out the front door the family upstairs was coming in. They're from India and even though it wasn't warm she was wearing a sari and sandals on her feet. Suddenly I felt sorry for her and reached into the bag.

"Here you are," I said making it seem like an everyday thing.

When she saw the fur coat the eyes nearly popped out of her head. She went to take it but her husband stopped her. He smiled at me. A slow sort of a smile. His teeth were very white.

"You are very kind," he said, "but you will need that coat for yourself."

"Oh no," I said quickly and just to let him know it wasn't a joke I pulled out the other coats.

"Look, I have plenty." And I smiled at him. His wife looked uneasy and the children tugged at her sari.

"We will not take your kind offer but thank you." This time I saw his smile was quick and with a touch of pity in it.

"Suit yourself," I said trying to sound as if it didn't

matter, but I felt hurt that they didn't want my surprise. It was then I realised that this was how hurt Tom must have felt when I didn't want all the lovely coats he kept bringing me as surprises.

So I screamed and kept on screaming until someone came. They still don't believe me when I tell them what happened, so they told me to simply write it down. All of it. So I'm doing that as best I can.

Tom never came back. No one knows where he is. I keep telling them I did nothing. You believe me don't you?

Maybe you think that as well as being a softie I'm gone a bit daft. You could be right. But you see Tom was the best thing that ever happened to me. I don't hold with all that Women's Lib stuff. People can get a job and be happy without a man if they like. I don't care. If that's their way. But it isn't mine. Men always like me and want me and that's nice. Maybe I could learn to be different. Maybe.

But then Tom could come back you know. He could.

Absence

Conleth O'Connor

IN THE NIGHT

           we were together but

when
morning
came

        THE DISTANCE BETWEEN US

was
visible
in the
sheets.

Clancy Wants Peace

By Criostoir O'Flynn

Clancy worked in a big flour mill on the docks, and he lived with his wife and nine children in a red-and-yellow Council house that was one in a block of eight, in a street of about eighty, in an estate of around eight hundred. So that the rumbling of machines in his ears all day, and the shouts, laughs and arguments on his hearth at night, made all his waking hours a long noisy blast composed of all things that are not peace and quiet.

In the early years of his manhood, Clancy, like most of his mates, sought relief from the toil of the day in the pub and the bookie's. Until the hungry mouths in the nest became so many that Clancy could only visit the pub at Christmas, and the bookie on nightmares.

So, from six to eleven nightly, Clancy stood to like a man, kept his sons to neutral corners, righted wrongs, and carpentered, cobbled, plumbed or barbered as the need arose.

Nightly towards eleven, the noises in the little

red-and-yellow house slowed, faded and ceased.   When he was finally alone in the cosy kitchen, Clancy would look around him in satisfaction.   From chairs and table and floor he would collect the pages of the newspaper, examine their numbers, and arrange them in order.   Then he would sit back deep in the wobbly old armchair beside the black iron range where the fire glowed behind iron bars, and say, nightly, "Ah, wisha -!"

For an hour, nightly, Clancy read.   Line by line he fished the black pools of print: news from the East, and from the West, Finance and Fashion, Racing and Sport, Births, Deaths and Marriages, Clancy proceeded steadily through them all, in peace profound.

At midnight, Clancy drank a final mug of tea, and then crept softly into the front parlour where his lawful wedded and weary wife was already snoring.

The nightly hour of peace and quiet was Clancy's substitute for the pleasures of the pub and the bookie's. Clancy never said it, but his wife knew it well.   And the family knew *their* side of it.   So that in the tidy little red-and-yellow house nobody or nothing would be allowed to disturb the peace on Clancy.

One night and the house quiet, the only sound the unheard ticking of the clock on the mantelpiece, Clancy secure in his enjoyment, he suddenly raised his head from the newspaper.   His hedgehog hair stood like wire and crooked harps wrinkled along his broad forehead.   When he heard the noise again, Clancy cocked up in his chair, listening like a condemned prisoner who heard the firing-squad at practice.

The scraping was as loud as a saw, as persistent as the bawl of a hungry child.   Staring at unseen horror, Clancy laid the newspaper gently, like a corpse, across his knees.

"A-a mouse!" Clancy whispered.   "In-in that press

there.

"A-a *mouse!*" he repeated, and the dainty sawing in the food press started up again as if to convince him.

"Oh Lord God above!" groaned Clancy. "There's an end to my bit of peace. And of course you *must* chew the timber, and the press bulging with food all around you! An' if only you'd wait till I was gone to bed, wouldn't it be all the same to you?"

"All right you little blackguard!" said Clancy, rising fearsomely to combat. "We'll soon see is it your house or mine!"

If he had seen him that night, Clancy would have minced the disturber with wallops of the poker. When he retired, almost an hour later than usual, Clancy had read only half the fashion page; not one solitary name had he studied on the Births, Deaths and Marriages, and there was his blue-and-white mug standing on the table with a grey scum on the cold tea in it ...

There was general worry in the house of Clancy the next night. The wife went exploring in the press of all-sorts, that was next-door neighbour to the tormented food press.

"I was full sure we had an old mousetrap in here," she said. " 'Tis here it would be if we had it."

"I'll catch him this night," declared Clancy, "if I have to follow him as far as New York. Is there no trap at all in the house?" he demanded.

His anger shot activity into all legs. One bright voice offered to run out next door and ask for the loan of a trap.

Even little Noreen, the trouble-maker, even *she* had gone quiet over in the corner between her father and the silent radio. Drawing in her exercise-copy she was, with her tongue like a raspberry through the corner of her mouth, drawing a big, upright, bewhiskered cat who was watching and waiting as a low, long-tailed mouseen came sneaking out of a hole in the corner ...

The magic hour of midnight was not far off when Clancy heard the mouse that night. On an ordinary night, he would just about then be contentedly filling his mug for the last time from the brown teapot. But to-night he had spent the hour since the family left him in strained listening and nervous jumpings. So that when the mouse *did* strike, it was a great relief to poor Clancy.

"So you're paying us another little call, are you now? Making your own house of it altogether, eh? Eat away so, eat away for yourself, my hero! I'm tellin' you there's a nice tasty morsel there under your snout that'll put a sudden stop to *your* gallop!"

The sawing suddenly stopped. Clancy stared at the door of the food press, listening with his very soul.

Peace.

After an agony of ten seconds, Clancy sprang and almost hauled the door from its hinges. There was no mouse to be seen; there was not a rustle or a movement in the press. On the floor was the expected tiny pile of gleaming sawdust, and over from it in a straight line stood the offering of fresh cheese, as apparent as the Alps.

"Five minutes to twelve!" moaned Clancy, as he dragged his weary bulk to the hearth. He bent and began to collect the scattered newspaper. "Whatever in the devil's name sent him in here to torment me! A little bit of peace and quiet, that's not much to ask, God knows now is it a lot, is it? All I want--" said Clancy, the paper folded and his body arching to drop back in the chair, "all I want is --"

Clancy stayed just as he was, bent up like a too-big leprechaun. The like of his gaping face was never seen in hell or heaven. Because *there* was the mouse on top of the black range.

There, right beside the bent-up Clancy, a little furry grey thing with a long twiny tail and glinting eyes, crouched on the black expanse of the range. And not idle or dancing was he, no, but eating. *Eating!*

Even through his daze, Clancy heard the loud shuffle of the newspaper as it drifted from his hands to lie around his feet. But the mouse took no notice; only moved a creep or two nearer to the fire side of the range, tasting further.

"Dripping!" whispered Clancy. "That's what he's after! Spatters of dripping on the range!"

Clancy dropped his eyes to locate the poker. Softly he folded himself down into his boots. The poker was on the floor inside the fender. Clancy reached and gripped it, not breathing. His rising was as gentle as the opening daisy. But the black top of the range was empty.

"Saints above, isn't he the limit! And I quieter than himself!"

Clancy dropped the poker and bounced to the food press, where he carefully took up the loaded trap. Back with him to the hearth, and there he arranged the trap in the dead centre of the black range. Then he stood back, panting more than he would after a heavy hour's bag-slinging in the flour mill. He poured his mug of tea and sat in to the table, sorely in need of the refreshment. His eyes strayed to the lump of cheese in the trap.

"Have it your own way so for a while, mousie," said Clancy, lifting his mug. "I'm going to bed, so you can die in peace. *Peace* says I!"

He had only said it when the mouse came again. Across from the inner corner of the range, straight across towards the bright, smelling cheese. The mouse stopped beside the trap. Clancy's eyes stood in his head. The mouse stirred his whiskers. Clancy was lifted out of his chair by the explosion.

His shaking hand still gripped the mug as the splashed tea warmed through his shirt. His two eyes stood out on sticks. The trap was upside down at one side of the black range. Over at the other side, the mouseen was tasting the lump of nicely toasted cheese...

Five winter nights after the first attack by the mouse, "We'll have to get a cat," said the wife, as she poured the tea.

"Is it a *cat*?" Clancy growled. "What about that last tiger we had? Howling and screeching out there in the back at all hours of the night and morning. Aren't we bad enough with a *mouse*, not to mind a *cat*?"

"Well," said the wife, looking to see if all the tea-cups were filled, "why don't you go and buy a bit of poison so? You know right well *that* would kill him for sure."

Clancy stopped buttering his bread.

"Poison!" he said, frowning, and the whole table shivered. "I wouldn't like to have that poison in the house at all."

All the little mouths were busy eating.

"Anyway," said Clancy, "we'll have another go with the trap to-night."

"Huh! The trap!" said the wife. "Sure you're trying that every night for a week now and you're getting no result, only torment and wearing yourself out. Everything you tried, every blessed thing, cheese, oatmeal, meat--it's maybe a pity we didn't put a drop of whiskey or something on them!"

Clancy laughed heartily. "Ha-Ha! That'd be all the same to him! Oh he's as cute as a fox! Look, five nights he's coming, and you never in all your life saw anything as bold and as --" Clancy changed his face suddenly, "May the devil sweep him away to hell out of here!"

The family had even learned to make somewhat less noise than usual between tea and bedtime. They were all pitying their father, and wondering at his great patience.

Good-night, sleep sound, good-night, angels keep ye, good night, good night ...

Clancy waited until the house was at peace. Then he took from the table the fragrant lump of cheese the wife had left ready for the trap. He broke it up small, *very* small, and put the little pieces where the top of the range was just nicely warm. The trap he placed unset on the fender. Then, Clancy sat back on his armchair, took up the newspaper confidently, and sighed with the old satisfaction, "Ah, wisha-!"

At the centre page he was when his visitor came that night. Clancy lowered the paper to his knees. He watched, grinning as the little mouse nibbled the warm cheese. Then he leaned forward and whispered, "A little drink now, Patsy, to wash it down. And don't forget to clean up the oul' whiskers! An' aren't you the devil-an-'all, you are indeed!"

When the mouse had eaten enough cheese, he ran along the copper pipe that led from behind the range to the sink in the corner near the window. He shinned up behind one of the taps. That tap was settled so as to have a regular drip available. The little mouse drank, washed his face and combed his whiskers, as cute as if he had taken lessons from the cat.

But Clancy had only an odd glance now for the antics of his mouseen. Lying back in the armchair in full satisfaction and peace, that's the way Clancy was, and he getting his sweet tooth deep into the contents of the sports page of the newspaper.

Pond
Máire Holmes

On a winter's day
in a remote area
near the bay.

I found you,
deep and rich
with still, dark waters.

A Love Poem
Shane Connaughton

I see you fading
In the grey December light
Your hair astreaming
In the sea-filled sky

Your feet becoming velvet
In the crying grass
Your face of beauty
Smiling like the sun

The soul of day is
Echoed in your eyes
Your breath of goodness
Sweeter than the wind

I love your gentle oneness with the earth
And pray love ripens though time grows great.

It Snowed That Night

Eamon Kelly

There were these two poets and they used to go every year to the winter fair in Kenmare to buy two cows for the tub. When the deal was done they'd tie the two cows to the lamp post and go into the pub, where they'd spend the day and portion of the night arguing, insulting people they didn't like and exchanging verses. When they'd come out bye an' bye they wouldn't be cold but the two cows would be perished. When they'd rip the ropes off their horns the cows'd gallop off to get the blood back in circulation.

Now, it so happened one year that the poets bought two black cows, and when they got out of the light of the town, the night was so dark and the cows so black that the poets couldn't see a splink. There they were with two ash plants running up and down, hether and over in gaps and out gates after the cows. They could only go by the sound, so when they heard anything they'd draw with the ash plants and were hitting one another as often as not.

They spent the night on the road, up bohereens and

into fields, and when it brightened in the morning they were driving two animals before them! Not their own I'm afraid. Two rangey bullocks belonging to some farmer in the Roughty Valley. By the time they had the bullocks restored to their rightful owners, by the time they had gone around to all the schools and made public the fact that the cows had strayed, and by the time they had found them they swore they would never again get into such a mix-up of an adventure if they could at all avoid it.

Time moved on and the winter fair in Kenmare came round again, and neighbours were surprised to see the two poets late at night in a public house and they maith go leor!

"It is none of our business," the neighbours remarked among themselves remembering the fools the poets made of themselves in the dark the year before. "Yerra let 'em at it!"

Drink or no drink you couldn't be ikey enough for poets. They got an inkling they were being talked about so one of 'em got up and sang,

> We don't give a tráithnín about darkness.
> Be it blacker than nature allows.
> We're prepared for it this time, my buckos.
> We've purchased two handsome white cows.

It snowed that night!

The Year's Ending

Sean Clarkin

We laid a wreath on your grave
and it was Christmas
and you
were not here.

When the year ended we
rejoiced
that it could do no more
damage

And when the new year began
we picked up the threads
of something that could no longer
be the same
without you.

Beginnings hurt
and endings
are seldom taken in their stride.

Many Years Ago

John B. Keane

Many years ago, in our street, there lived an old woman who had but one son who's name was Jack. Jack's father had died when Jack was no more than a gorsoon but Jack's mother went out to work to support her son and herself.

As Jack grew older she still went out and worked for the good reason that Jack did not like work. The people in the street used to say that Jack was only good for three things. He was good for eating, he was good for smoking, and he was good for drinking. Now to give him his due he never beat his mother or abused her verbally. All he did was to skedaddle to England when she was too old to go out to work. Years passed but she never had a line from her only son. Every Christmas she would stand inside her window waiting for a card or a letter. She waited in vain.

When Christmas came to our street it came with a loud laugh and an expansive humour that healed old wounds and lifted the hearts of young and old. If the Christmas that came to our street were a person he would be something like this: he would be in his sixties but glowing with rude health. His face would be flushed and chubby with sideburns down to the rims of his jaws. He would be wearing gaiters and a tweed suit and he would be mildly intoxicated. His pockets would be filled with silver coins for small boys and girls and for the older folk he would have a party at which he would preside with his waist-coated paunch, extending benignly, and his posterior benefiting from the glow of a roaring log fire.

There would be scalding punch for everybody and there would be roast geese and ducks, their beautiful golden symmetries exposed in large dishes and tantalising gobs of potato-stuffing oozing and bursting from their rear-end stitches. There would be singing and storytelling and laughter and perhaps a tear here and there when absent friends were toasted. There would be gifts for everybody and there would be great good will, as neighbours embraced, promising to cherish each other truly till another twelve months had passed.

However, Christmas is an occasion and not a person. A person can do things, change things, create things but all our occasions are only what we want them to be. For this reason Jack's mother waited, Christmas after Christmas, for word of her wandering boy. To other houses would come stout, registered envelopes from distant loved ones who remembered. There would be bristling, crumply envelopes from America with noble rectangular cheques to delight the eye and comfort the soul. There would be parcels and packages of all shapes and sizes so that every house became a warehouse until the great day came when all goods would be distributed.

Now it happened that in our street there was a postman who knew a lot more about his residents than they knew about themselves. When Christmas came he was weighted with bags of letters and parcels. People awaited his arrival the way children awaited a bishop on confirmation day. He was not averse to indulging in a drop of the comforts wherever such comforts were tendered but comforts or not the man was always sensitive to the needs of others. In his heart resided the spirit of Christmas. Whenever he came to the house where the old woman lived he would crawl on all fours past the windows. He just didn't have the heart to go by and be seen by her. He hated to disappoint people, particularly old people. For the whole week before Christmas she would take up her position behind the faded curtains, waiting for the letter which never came.

Finally the postman could bear it no longer. On Christmas Eve he delivered to our house a mixed bunch of cards and letters. Some were from England. He requested one of these envelopes when its contents were removed. He re-wrote the name and address and he also wrote a short note which he signed "your loving son, Jack." Then from his pocket he extracted a ten shilling note, a considerable sum in those far off days. He placed the note in the envelope. There was no fear the old woman would notice the handwriting because if Jack was good at some things, as I have already mentioned, he was not good at other things and one of these was writing. When the postman came to the old woman's door he knocked loudly. When she appeared he put on his best official voice and said:

"Sign for this if you please, Missus."

The old woman signed and opened the envelope. The tears appeared in her eyes and she cried out loud.

"I declare to God but Jack is a scholar."

"True for you," said the postman.

"I always knew there was good in him," she said. "I always knew it."

"There's good in everyone Missus," said the postman as he moved on to the next house.

The street was not slow in getting the message and in the next and last post there were many parcels for the old woman. It was probably the best Christmas the street ever had.

The Christmas Train
Michael O'Sullivan

I stand by the table and watch the train
speed round the tiny track.
Your fingers are the roots of an old tree
your smile its young blossoms
which spring no matter what its age may be.
I come to you each time
because I never wind it properly,
wrecked in transit from the north-pole you say
and stare right through its steel.
Now it is weeks later, and the train returns
guided by your stubble fingers.
It speeds around the schoolroom window
and gets trapped on the ropes.
I sit and watch the ghostly train away
while asked the question for the second time,
wrecked in transit from the north-pole I say.

A Christmas Story
(A Precocious Child)
Maeve Binchy

When I was young and spoiled and indulged, instead of being old and spoiled and indulged, I decided late one Christmas Eve that I was going to cancel all previous letters to Santa Claus and ask him for a doll's house.

Laboriously and apologetically I wrote all this to himself and put it up the chimney and retired happily, leaving confusion and sadness amongst those who had bought me a lovely blackboard and fifty pieces of chalk.

A child's Christmas couldn't be ruined, they told each other, but on the other hand all the shops were closed and doll's houses were out. So they tried to make one. For hours and hours, I believe, they laboured on a big box and painted it white and drew windows in it and stuck on chimneys that kept falling off. One of the few rows of their married life developed over the inability to construct a simple thing like a doll's house.

"Boys should have learned carpentry at school," said

my mother in despair as the front of the house caved in yet again.

"Women should know about toys," countered my father as he got out the glue pot once more.

Then they thought about straw and making a doll's house, Hawaiian style, but this might not be a good idea in case I hadn't heard of Polynesian houses.

"With all the money we pay at that expensive school, they should have taught her that," said my father. But the straw was damp anyway, so that was abandoned.

A doll's igloo with cotton wool as snow was considered and abandoned. A doll's tepee seemed a good idea if they could paint a doll up as an Indian to go with it. But it required bark, skins, or canvas, and so they had to give that up, too, since they had been thinking of making it with a sheet.

They ruminated wistfully about my younger sister then, and now, easier to please in life, who would be delighted with a rattle or a teddy bear or even nothing at all.

"To be fair," said my father, "she *is* only two. Maeve is six."

"I wonder is it normal for a six-year-old to want a doll's house anyway," said my mother. So they had another hour looking up Normal-Six-Year-Olds in Dr. Spock or its equivalent, decided it was boringly normal and inconvenient, and went back to work.

They got bricks and stones in from the garden. They looked up a book called *One Thousand Things a Boy Can Do*, but none of them included making a doll's house. My father became interested in one of the things a boy could do which was digging a tunnel in the garden to irrigate the flower beds.

"That's all we need on Christmas Day," said my mother wearily, "for the neighbours to see you irrigating the flower beds with tunnels."

It was nearly dawn. The fat cherub was asleep with no idea of anything being amiss. They came into my room, set up the blackboard and wrote a note on it with one of the pieces of chalk!

Dear Maeve, your chimney is too narrow and I can't get the doll's house down it. Please do not be upset. It will arrive as an extra gift sometime in January. You have been a good girl. All the reindeer are asking for you. Love from Santa Claus.

It was morning, and with shining eyes I was beating on them begging them to wake up. After only two hours' sleep this wasn't easy for them to do. They showed great alarm. Was I going to threaten to leave home! Were there tears and tantrums which would spoil the day for everyone! Not at all.

"You'll never believe it," I said. "Santa Claus wrote me a note. In his own writing. It's on an old blackboard or something, but it's obviously very valuable. Nobody has seen Santa Claus's writing before. We'll have to show it to everyone. We might lend it to a museum."

It was a good Christmas, like all our Christmases were together; the only thing that makes me sad at this time of the year is that I may have forgotten to tell them that...but perhaps they knew.

Final Whistle

Greg Delanty

We sat on the magic carpet of a prickly rug
decorated with tassels and cigarette burns.
I can still see your ugly, nicotined fingers
wrap a chipped, Chelsea soccer mug
and catch a whiff of porter
off your laughing breath.

How come I always won
playing Three Goals In with you and Uncle John?
I was Bobby Charlton, John was Gordon Banks,
but who were you?
You'd recall being almost drowned in Youghal
swimming out to retrieve a football.

Once when I shot wide
we watched our plastic 1966 World Cup ball
float from sight.
That night I grieved
for it drifting
in such a pitch.

Last night
I dreamt of a boy

in the dazzling spotlight of the sun
shining along the water
and heard him call to his father:
Look the sea's brought back our ball.
I woke as the years fell like the waves.
The wind whistled a relentless cat call.

Copyright Acknowledgements

For permission to reprint copyright material, the editor and publishers are grateful to the following:

Title verse taken from the poem "*A Page Falls Open*" reprinted by kind permission of the author from "*The Year of the Knife*" by Philip Casey (The Raven Arts Press, 1991).

"*Sunflower*" reprinted by kind permission of Bloodaxe Books Ltd. from "*Hail! Madam Jazz*" by Micheal O'Siadhail (Bloodaxe Books, 1992).

"*Hello*" copyright Michael Durack, 1993.

"*Tiger's Bay*" an extract reprinted by kind permission of the author and BBC Northern Ireland from "*A Word In Your Ear*" by Sam McAughtry and Albert Crawford (BBC NI, 1990).

"*The Blue Boat*" reprinted by kind permission of the author and the Gallery Press from "*The Rainmakers*" by Francis Harvey (The Gallery Press, 1988).

"*Holy Water and the German Bomb*" copyright Joe O'Donnell, 1993. Adapted from a piece first broadcast on Sunday Miscellany, RTE Radio One.

"*My Neighbour*" copyright Morgan Llywelyn, 1993.

"*Have You Forgotten?*" copyright Kathleen Kierse, 1993.

"*Washing Up and Black Puddings*" an adapted version of a story from *Patterns* by Eithne Strong (Poolbeg Press, 1980). Originally published in the Irish Press, New Irish Writing, edited by David Marcus, 1968. Copyright Eithne Strong, 1993.

"*Becoming a Citizen*" reprinted by kind permission of the author from "*The Year of the Knife*" by Philip Casey (The Raven Arts Press, 1991).

"*All Wet Days*" reprinted by kind permission of the author from "*The Way We Are*" by Alice Taylor, 1983.

"*A Daughter's Duty*" copyright Emma Cooke, 1993.

"*Lifelines*" reprinted by kind permission of the author and the Gallery Press from "*Oven Lane*" by Michael Coady (Gallery Press, 1987).

"*Writing*" reprinted with the kind permission of the author from "*Long Tongue*" by Anne LeMarquand Hartigan (Beaver Row Press, 1982).